Davidson
2004

SAINTS AND THE AUDIENCE IN MIDDLE ENGLISH
BIBLICAL DRAMA

Chester N. Scoville

Saints and the Audience in Middle English Biblical Drama

UNIVERSITY OF TORONTO PRESS
Toronto Buffalo London

© University of Toronto Press Incorporated 2004
Toronto Buffalo London
Printed in Canada

ISBN 0-8020-8944-5

Printed on acid-free paper

National Library of Canada Cataloguing in Publication

Scoville, Chester N. (Chester Norman), 1968–
  Saints and the audience in Middle English biblical drama / Chester
N. Scoville.

  Includes bibliographical references and index.
  ISBN 0-8020-8944-5

  1. Mysteries and miracle-plays, English – History and criticism.   2. Bible
plays, English – History and criticism.   3. Christian drama, English
(Middle) – History and criticism.   4. English drama – To 1500 – History and
criticism.   5. Theater – England – History – Medieval, 500–1500.   6. Theater
audiences – England – History – To 1500.   I. Title.

PR641.S36 2004   822'.051609   C2004-902846-4

University of Toronto Press acknowledges the financial assistance to its
publishing program of the Canada Council for the Arts and the Ontario
Arts Council.

This book has been published with the help of a grant from the Canadian
Federation for the Humanities and Social Sciences, through the Aid to
Scholarly Publications Programme, using funds provided by the Social
Sciences and Humanities Research Council of Canada.

University of Toronto Press acknowledges the financial support for its
publishing activities of the Government of Canada through the Book
Publishing Industry Development Program (BPIDP).

Contents

Acknowledgments

This book, which has been curiously long in coming, owes its existence to many people. Thanks are due to Alexandra F. Johnston, David N. Klausner, and Suzanne Akbari, for shepherding it through its initial form; to Brian Corman, Clifford Davidson, Michael Dixon, JoAnna Dutka, David Galbraith, and Dan White for invaluable advice; and most of all to Kimberley M. Yates for advice and support far above any reasonable call of duty. Thanks go also to Suzanne Rancourt, Clare Orchard, Barbara Porter, and Doug Hildebrand of the University of Toronto Press.

Any errors that remain are entirely my own responsibility, and may be put down to the author's sloth or stubbornness, as the reader chooses.

SAINTS AND THE AUDIENCE IN MIDDLE ENGLISH
BIBLICAL DRAMA

1
Medieval Drama and Community Identity

In the York Cycle's play 'The Temptation,' the audience is shown a difference not only between good and evil but also between two different views of themselves. The Devil, Diabolus, holds the audience in contempt, with little regard for either their individuality or their community, muscling them out of the way as he enters, dismissively calling them 'all þis þrang' and wishing, 'high myght зou hang/Right with a rope' (York 22/2–4).[1] He sees the audience as his victims, unable either to do good or to be secure:

> And I haue ordayned so þam forne
>   None may þame fende,
> Þat fro all likying ar they lorne
>   Withowten ende.   (York 22/15–18)

Not only this, but he also, crucially, dismisses their ability to manipulate discourse, saying,

> And nowe sum men spekis of a swayne,
> Howe he schall come and suffre payne
> And with his dede to blisse agayne
>   Þei schulde be bought.
> But certis þis tale is but a trayne,
>   I trowe it noзt.   (York 22/19–24)

Such is the Devil's view of humanity and of the audience: morally helpless, unable to speak sense to each other, able therefore only to be a throng of undifferentiated victims or passive spectators.

Christ, on the other hand, shows a quite different point of view when he speaks of the audience. He concludes the play by affirming the audience's own moral capacities: 'ouercome schall þei noȝt be/ Bot yf þay will' (York 22/197–8). Furthermore, he promises,

> My blissing haue þei with my hande
> Þat with swilke greffe is noȝt grucchand,
> And also þat will stiffely stande
>   Agaynste þe fende.   (York 22/205–8)

To stiffly stand, as Christ puts it here, is not to stand passively by but to resist; it is to endure in one's conscience the temptations of greed, fame, and power, as he has just done before the audience during the course of the play. He affirms, in fact, 'Þare myrroure may þei make of me' (York 22/195). In short, he affirms that each member of the audience may, in emulating him, act as one in resisting evil, and therefore in behaving ethically and decently to each other.

In this play, one can see in miniature the basic issues surrounding the good characters of medieval drama: the importance of moral action and the belief that the audience is capable of it; the balance between the individual conscience and the community acting as a whole; the belief that narrative and rhetoric – potentially, the binding language of a community – can be useful in achieving these goals; and, always of crucial importance in medieval Europe, the *imitatio Christi* as a way of anchoring moral action. This last aspect of the play focuses attention not only on Christ himself, but also on the main subject of this study, his imitators the saints: role models for the audience in the task of achieving moral action and sanctity in life.

For the medieval Christian, saints occupied a border point between the concrete life of the earthly community – the Church Militant – and the ultimate community – the Church Triumphant, or the Communion of Saints. This duality of existence lies at the heart of the cult of the saints. It exists also as a problem to be confronted in attempts to portray the saints artistically. A clear statement of the challenge may be found in the fifteenth-century English *Dives and Pauper*: '[Y]magis stondinge in chirchis mai be considered in two wyses, eþir as þei representen þe state of seintis of whom þei ben ymagis as þei lyuyden in þis lijf ... or ellis þei mai be considerid as þei representen þe state of endeles blisse ... Neþeles in al such peinture an onest meen ... is to be kept, for seyntis louyden an onest meen in al her lyuyng.'[2] It is well established that defenders of medieval biblical plays used such traditions of sacred visual art as an analogy for the function of plays. In particular, they argued that audiences 'seinge the passioun of Crist and of his seintis, ben movyd to compassion and devocion' and that such matters 'ben holden in mennes mind' by the dramatic experience.[3] Compassion, a social virtue, and devotion, an internal one, stick in the memories of ordinary people through contemplation of those who occupy the balance point between the temporal and the eternal. An 'onest meen' indeed!

Not only in theory but also in practice, medieval audiences experienced biblical plays as aspects of both devotion and community. This fact was constant in different cities and over the period of the plays' history. As the A/Y Memorandum Book declared in 1399, shortly after the beginning of vernacular plays in England, York's plays were 'en honour & reuerence nostreseignour Iesu Crist & honour & profitt de mesme la Citee (in honour and reverence of our Lord Jesus Christ and for the glory and benefit of the same city);[4] over a century later, the Chester Proclamation of 1531–2 says that its plays were 'not only for the Augmentation & incres<...>faith of o<...>suyor iesu Crist & to exort the myndes of the common people<...> doctryne th<...>f but also for the commenwelth & prosperitie of this Citie.'[5] Nor is the prosperity mentioned in both records of a purely or even primarily economic sort: 'the value of cooperation and mutuality in seeking salvation'[6] underlies manifold activities in towns, cities, and parishes in the late Middle Ages, and, given the corporate nature of the drama, may reasonably be assumed to underlie it as well.

The community was important not only in providing the material means for producing the plays, but also in ensuring that the individual audience members' responses to the plays should remain orthodox; late medieval corporate Christianity was a framework that both enabled and defined the experience available to any given spectator or participant.[7] To a (post)modern mind, such universality of ideology is, and should be, troubling. Yet, paradoxically, it is not through conformity of identity that medieval plays achieve their goals. The basic emotive response that the playwrights seek, compassion, is based upon the individual remaining individual while at the same time comprehending the experiences and emotions of other individuals. In other words, the playwrights sought to ignite not empathy or conformity, but sympathy. While empathy (the word literally means 'into-feeling') implies a unification between individuals, sympathy or compassion (both words mean literally 'with-feeling') implies a parallel set of feelings and experiences between two distinct individuals.[8]

Such experiences of compassion are at the heart of much late medieval piety. For instance, Nicholas Love's *Mirror of the Blessed Life of Jesus Christ* urges its readers to imagine themselves, as themselves, in compassionate companionship with biblical figures: 'Now lat vs here go with hem by deuout contemplation, & help we to bere þat blessed birþen þe child Jesus in oure soule by deuocioun.'[9] Similarly, such mystics as Margery Kempe and Julian of Norwich spoke in the same terms. Margery Kempe speaks, for instance, of imagining herself going 'wyth owyr Lady to Bedlem,' paying for the pregnant Virgin's lodgings, finding food for her, and weeping over the newly born Christ child.[10] Julian reflects on several of her visions in like terms, for instance: 'Me thought I wolde haue bene that tyme with mary Mawdeleyne and with othere that were Crystes loverse, that I myght have sene bodylye the passionn of oure lorde that he sufferede for me, that I myght have sufferede with hym as othere dyd that lovyd hym.'[11] In the participation in, and beholding of, biblical plays, the people of late medieval English towns have the chance as a whole community to be with these figures, to see them, to go with them, to suffer with them, and even to provide financially for them and their journeys. These reactions of practical compassion and devotion enabled individuals, while remaining themselves, to act in community with each other by acting in communion with the biblical figures who inspired them.

The triggers for such inspiration lie first of all within the culture surrounding late medieval life, which was centred around the church. The assumptions of the medieval Christian religion can be said to have constituted a normative system of beliefs, through which people quite naturally interpreted their lives. But such a system must be maintained in order to function, and people must be persuaded to act upon their beliefs. This is where the aesthetic and rhetorical devices of the medieval plays become of interest, because it is through these persuasive devices that the medieval playwrights attempted to strengthen and activate the matrix of compassion and devotion that defined their culture's highest ideals.

Of course, the playwrights were aware that rhetoric is a dangerous tool, as many of the finest minds since Plato have maintained. They were also aware that, in order to move their audience most effectively, they must appeal to the emotions as well as to the intellect: that they must argue by inciting passion (*pathos*) and by showing the speaker's fine character (*ethos*), and not merely through the more reputable method of logical argument (*logos*). Although *ethos* and *pathos* may be, and sometimes have been, seen rather as the down-at-heels cousins of *logos*, nonetheless to argue by logic alone may end up in mere intellectualism, the kind of aridity that Augustine warned against:

> Illi animos audientium in errorem moventes impellentesque dicendo terreant contristent exhilarent exhortentur ardenter, isti pro veritate lenti frigidique dormitent. Quis ita desipiat ut hoc sapiat?

> That [preachers of falsehood], pushing and propelling their listeners' minds towards error, would speak so as to inspire fear, sadness, and elation, and issue passionate exhortations, while we, in the name of truth, can only idle along sounding dull and indifferent. Who could be so senseless as to find this sensible?[12]

But the medieval playwrights did indeed appeal to the whole person, and did so by co-opting the most effective tools of rhetoric for the saintly; they thus created a tool for moving an audience to virtuous living in community with others.

This book argues that the techniques used by medieval playwrights to create characters were rhetorical in nature; that the central characters of the plays are the saints, the heroes, and the virtuous; and that the function of these central characters was, as already discussed, to unite the community of the audience in its desire for holy living. It is curious that these arguments need to be made this late in the day. After all, the study of medieval drama as an academic discipline is now nearly two centuries old; the revival of medieval drama in modern performance is over fifty years old. Too often, however, the assumptions of early modernism coloured the perceptions of our criticism of these plays, with the result that villains such as Herod have taken centre stage in much of our thinking when we regard medieval plays. Indeed, medieval plays contain much that is lurid, much that is gruesome, and indeed much that is verisimilar to life; all literature and drama do so. But the focus on these aspects in medieval plays has, I believe, led to a merely partial understanding of their nature, a distortion that only recently has started to be corrected.[13]

The result of this distortion is the attitude that the villains are the most realistic, therefore interesting, of the characters on stage. The plays, to their supporters, can then be said to be subversive,[14] or proto-

Brechtian,[15] or evidence of a growing impulse toward realism and humanism,[16] or to possess any number of anti-authoritarian virtues. To their detractors – medieval and modern – the plays can be said to be primitive, vulgar, monkish, or superstitious, or to possess any number of unthinkingly collectivist vices. These are the logical outcomes of much of our critical tradition, yet the fact remains that modern critics do not universally think this way about these plays. In fact, many contemporary critics – and many contemporary audiences – see these plays in the way that their creators and original audiences surely did: as persuasive to goodness and as a powerful communal experience. It therefore behoves us to continue to develop our critical vocabulary for saying so; a step in that continuance is the aim of this book.

For the saints of medieval plays are both central and fascinating. Among the most interesting and powerful of the saints that the medieval playwrights portrayed are four flawed human beings who nonetheless achieved sainthood: Thomas the Doubter, Mary Magdalene, Joseph, and Paul. These four figures occupy liminal spaces between faith and doubt, virtue and vice, humanity and sanctity. In them, as portrayed in the plays, the medieval audience found not only role models but also ways of bringing divine qualities into their own lives, uniting them in their common humanity and in their religious aspirations. Furthermore, the medieval dramatic portrayals of these four saints demonstrate the varied methods of the playwrights, as well as their exploration of the limits of language, drama, and their ability to accomplish their goals.

Thomas finds himself, in all four of his Middle English incarnations, in the centre of a conflict not only over the nature of the resurrection but also of the ability of logic and language to function as persuasive tools. The plays of Thomas, involved as they are with one of the most puzzling of the Christian mysteries, interweave the issues of resurrection, rhetoric, and solidarity with others. They point to the limitations of *logos* as a persuasive device, and emphasize the importance of emotional persuasion and understanding, pointing the way to a panegyric rhetoric capable of moving an audience to a united experience of wonder. They also demonstrate both the necessity and the limitations of the individual quest for truth, and posit a way between the excesses of collective dogmatism and autonomous individualism in the field of ontology.

Mary Magdalene, in the Digby play of her life, is an embodiment of exactly this type of rhetoric, and functions, appropriately, as a unifying force for the people among whom she moves. She also, however, stands at the centre of a play concerned with one of the key issues in any community: the proper use and legitimate origin of authority. Thus, the Digby play of Mary Magdalene also explores the importance of ethical appeal and of the character of authority, while crafting a portrait of the saint that defies much modern expectation.

Existing on the outer edge of society, far from the centres of authority, Joseph, in his portrayal in the York Cycle, comes across as a representative of the audience: the ultimate exemplar of 'natural man,' as he has been called.[17] Yet he is more complex than that: the intermediary between the audience and the mystery of the incarnation. Apparently on the margins, he draws the audience together to focus on a centre that is greater than himself. His story is among the most effective uses of emotion – *pathos* – in the corpus of Middle English drama, and as such represents a fine example of the participatory, sympathetic nature of community as participation in mystery.

Finally, Paul, in the Digby play of his life, shows us in miniature a perfectly balanced example of rhetoric as communal action and experience. Not surprisingly, the portrait of the church's seminal writer and community builder epitomizes all the processes of participatory rhetoric at work in the medieval portraits of the saints.

These four figures between them map out the basic issues and methods that underlie the rhetoric of the saintly in medieval drama, and provide us with a guide to understanding the rhetoric that united community. One might ask, logically enough, why should we not go further and study the rhetoric of God – the central character, after all, in all the biblical plays, and the one to whom all the others point? The answer is simply that one has to begin somewhere, and, following the lead of much medieval Christianity, this study proceeds from the earthly – from the clearer traces of imperfect humanity's struggle to understand and communicate.

2

Thomas and the Limits of Rhetoric

'Doubting Thomas' has become a byword for the rational, sceptical, individual seeker of truth. Refusing to be cowed by his peers, refusing to accept emotional outbursts of faith as evidence, Thomas is possibly the most sympathetic of the apostles from a modern standpoint. Of course, truth is revealed to him in the end; but the question remains, is that revelation a result of his doubts or in spite of his doubts? This is one of the issues that the plays of Thomas explore; their answer, nearly uniformly, comes in their revelation of their own inadequacy as *logos*. The plays of Thomas demonstrate the limitations of persuasive rhetoric as medieval playwrights saw them: undermining the possibility of abstract logical discourse as a conduit to ultimate truth, acknowledging the individual quest for truth as a necessary but merely preliminary step, and pointing to a communal, affective, physical experience as the final source of truth, the plays give us a model for viewing their writers' understanding and expectation of their own project in persuading and moving their audiences.

Thomas, after all, exists in a liminal space between faith and doubt; his story therefore presents an opportunity for playwrights to help the audience community to negotiate similar spaces in their own lives. The proverbial figure of 'Doubting Thomas,' however, is too simple for effective drama, too flat to be sympathetic – and sympathy is key to understanding how medieval dramatic rhetoric worked. Thomas is therefore fleshed out in the biblical plays of late medieval England; much of his character is drawn from the theological and aesthetic implications of medieval views of the Incarnation and Resurrection. In addition, his interaction with Jesus, Mary Magdalene, and the other Apostles in the plays serves both to move the audience to faith and, paradoxically, to demonstrate the parameters, limitations, and function of Christian rhetoric as the playwrights conceived of them: a rhetoric illuminated by, though not constrained by, classical and Augustinian rhetorics.

The sources for Thomas's character are both scriptural and patristic. In the Gospels, Thomas appears in all lists of the twelve apostles, but is most distinguished from his fellows in the Gospel of John. His first words in that Gospel come immediately before the raising of Lazarus, and are themselves a foreshadowing of Christ's own death: 'Tunc ergo dixit eis Iesus manifeste: Lazarus mortuus est. Et gaudeo propter vos, ut credatis, quoniam non eram ibi: sed eamus ad eum. Dixit ergo Thomas, qui dicitur Didymus, ad condiscipulos: Eamus et nos, ut moriamur cum eo' (Then therefore Jesus said to them plainly: Lazarus is dead. And I am glad, for your sakes, that I was not there, that you may believe: but let us go to him. Thomas therefore, who is called Didymus, said to his fellow disciples: Let us also go, that we may die with him. [John 11:14–16])[1] In the same Gospel, Thomas at the Last Supper asks the question, 'Domine, nescimus quo vadis; et quomodo possumus viam scire? (Lord, we know not whither thou goest; and how can we know the way? [John 14:5]) and receives the crucial answer, 'Ego sum via, et veritas, et vita' (I am the way, and the truth, and the life [John 14:6]). Most famously, of course, Thomas doubts the truth of the Resurrection.

As skeletal as the accounts of Thomas are, in all three of his major appearances he is connected immediately to the problems of Christ's death and resurrection, and to the problem of how Christians should live. Unsurprisingly, this biblical association of a shadowy, marginal figure with questions of central importance led to patristic interpretation, both of the meaning of Thomas's and Jesus' actual words, and of Thomas's character and state of mind.

In all of the Middle English plays of Thomas, the precise nature of his doubt is key to the unfolding of plot and the revelation of character. Consideration of the plays' *inventio* consists largely in interpretation of the nature of that doubt, which is not clear from the plays' key source text. The biblical Thomas says merely, 'Non credam' (I will not believe [John 20:25]). He does not specify exactly *what* he will not believe; the details were left up to the theologian and the playwright. In the plays, his disbelief is not so simple as disbelieving the resurrection; rather, it has to do with fairly precise theological thinking about the resurrection. Thomas, rather than being a figure of generic doubt, despair, or cynicism (in other words, rather than being a 'doubting Thomas'), is instead incredulous of only one thing: the resurrection of the body.

The other contrast that shapes the plays is that between corporeal and noncorporeal explanations of resurrection. Perhaps the bluntest biblical assertion of bodily resurrection is to be found in Job: 'Et rursum circumdabor pelle mea, et in carne mea videbo Deum (And I shall be clothed again with my skin, and in my flesh I shall see God [Job 19:26]). The doctrine of bodily resurrection was central to Christianity from the beginning; in the late Middle Ages, it took on particular significance with the general emphasis on corporeality in popular piety. In the visual arts, portrayals of the very episode we are considering show a positive fascination with the subject, with Christ often seizing Thomas's hand and pulling it towards his wounds.[2] Such fascination was not, however, morbid.[3] Rather, 'for all its gross physicality, its function was spiritual, to bring home to the spectator the reality of his own mortality, and thereby to bring him to a sense of the urgency of his own need for conversion. More immediately, it was designed to evoke fellow-feeling and pity'[4] for the suffering or dead, and, since everyone suffers and dies, with the community as a whole. Thus the combination of key *topoi* that shape the plays' doctrine – that the Resurrection is both miraculous and corporeal – existed in contexts of both scholarly speculation and popular, communal piety. The play, with its combination of logical argument and alogical, emotional assertion, can be seen as an exploration of the two.

The importance of the physicality of Christ for popular piety has been argued numerous times; the rhetorical implications of it as a species of proof are also important, however. Aristotle argues that '[o]f the modes of persuasion some belong strictly to the art of rhetoric and some do not. By the latter I mean such things as are not supplied by the speaker but are there at the outset – witnesses, evidence given under torture, written contracts, and so on.'[5] Thus Christ's provision of physical evidence following the failure of the Apostles to convince Thomas seems to set limits on the power of rhetoric in the realm of faith. Accordingly, the plays of Thomas explore the limitations of human language and the functions thereof. Such a project might seem to undercut their very function. As we shall see, however, once they have made their exploration they also skilfully suggest a way out of the trap they seem to set for themselves by pointing the way to an incarnational rhetoric rather different from its classical predecessors.

The most unusual and the longest – and rhetorically one of the most complex – of the Thomas plays is the Towneley version. This is not a well-loved or frequently cited play; Eleanor Prosser's evaluation of it as 'an illustration of some of the serious faults to which revisers of the fifteenth century were prone'[6] is a succinct enough statement of its alleged merit that no further assessment seems needed. Yet it is far more sophisticated than it seems at first glance.

Thomas in Towneley is a well-meaning man of faith who suffers from a specific form of spiritual blindness, one that makes him unable to accept the resurrection of the body in the state of mind in which he finds himself. His blind spot is established immediately upon his entrance, when he is confronted with the other disciples' claims and speaks quite precisely regarding his doubts:

> Let be for shame! Apartly,
> Fantom dyssauys the.
> Ye sagh hym not bodely;
> His gost it myght well be.   (Towneley 28/321–4)[7]

Thomas does not doubt that the Apostles may have seen Christ after his death. Nor does he doubt that Christ may have come to comfort them in spirit; in fact, he seems to think it a likely possibility. He also does not make light of their 'aduersyté'; in fact, it is he who asks them to take their own grief more seriously than he thinks they are taking it. Nor, in this play, is he the only one to doubt the resurrection of the body. The disbelief of the Apostles at the play's outset focuses on the same specific doctrine:

> [*Petrus.*] It is som spirite or els som gast;
> Othere was it noght.
> We may trow on no kyns wise
> That ded man may to lyfe ryse;
> This then is oure thoght.   (Towneley 28/9–13)

A key difference, in fact, is that Peter speaks only of 'som spirite'; he does not guess that it might be Jesus' own ghost sent for comfort, as Thomas later does. Furthermore, the basis for the Apostles' disbelief of Mary Magdalene and the basis for Thomas's disbelief of Peter are quite different from each other.

The Apostles base their disbelief of Mary Magdalene's account on a distrust of her character; this distrust is expressed in terms of antifeminist satire. Indeed, Paul, often seen as the prototypical antifeminist of the Church, is present in person[8] despite the play's chronology to make the point about women's untrustworthiness:

> And it is wretyn in oure law,
> 'There is no trust in womans saw,
> No trust faith to belefe;
> For with thare quayntyse and thare gyle
> Can thay laghe and wepe somwhile,
> And yit nothyng theym grefe.'   (Towneley 28/29–34)

The Pauline letters, of course, contain influential statements against women's preaching (1 Cor. 14:35, 1 Tim. 2:11–12), but the antifeminist tradition was not solely dependent on those. The play's most recent editors suggest that Paul's rebuke here depends far more on contemporary preaching than upon actual Pauline writings.[9] Woolf argues that this fashionable antifeminism 'serves the same purpose as [...] in the plays of Joseph's Doubts,'[10] that is, to provide a contrast between the miracle of incarnation and 'the satirical *fabliau* style of the fallen world.'[11] But Paul is not referring to any *fabliaux* but to the sermon tradition; furthermore, he explicitly refers to texts, not oral tradition as Woolf suggests. It is striking that Paul insists so strongly upon 'oure law,' an attitude more commonly associated in Middle English drama with the tyrants of the Passion, especially Annas and Caiaphas. Similarly, his elaboration, 'In oure bookes this fynde we wretyn – /All manere of men well it wyttyn – ' (Towneley 28/35–6) echoes the smugness of the Doctors in the Temple whom Christ rebukes at the beginning of his ministry.

Paul is relying above all upon a series of maxims about the nature of certain forms of human being. This is a particular body of rhetorician's lore that originates with Aristotle's catalogue of human types in book 2 of the *Rhetoric* but finds its fullest expression in the Middle Ages with the *Pastoral Care* of Gregory the Great.[12] But rather than pursuing the Aristotelian or Gregorian purpose of such categorization – judging the best way to address an audience so categorized – Paul instead uses it to judge the trustworthiness of a speaker, her *ethos*. This is, as we shall see, an issue of central importance to the character of Mary Magdalene in the Digby play devoted to her.

Thomas, on the other hand, bases his disbelief of Peter not on a general assessment of Peter's character but on questioning of Peter's current state of mind:

Whannow, Peter, art thou mad? ...
Thou hym forsoke, so was thou rad,
When they to the can speke.   (Towneley 28/305–7)

Even Thomas's reference to Peter's betrayal of Jesus does not focus on
any traitorous nature in Peter, but on the state of mind he was in at the
time. The distinction between Thomas's assessment of Peter and Paul's
assessment of Mary Magdalene is that between two species of characterization (*ethopoeia*) as practised in rhetorical training of the late Middle Ages: one focused on 'general character or habit of mind,' while the
other focused on 'the immediate emotions occasioned by a given situation.'[13] Thomas's concern is entirely with the latter; he speaks not only
of Peter's state of mind but his own, and notes the impossibility of
belief as he is:

Thou has answerd me full wele
And full skylfully,
Bot my hart is harde as stele
To trow in sich mastry.   (Towneley 28/385–8)

Thus Thomas is concerned with the present emotional situation, not
with general statements of character: with the latter species of *ethopoeia*, not the former.

A focus on emotion allows Thomas to escape some of the more cyni-
cal ways of viewing humanity, namely, those that focus on unchange-
ability of character. Paul's remarks to Mary Magdalene suggest that
she is inevitably untrustworthy, that her sinful nature is inherent and
unchangeable; Thomas's rebuke to Peter, by contrast, suggests that his
upset state of mind is temporary. In addition, Thomas admits that his
own state of mind, stirred up as it is, is at least potentially changeable.

Thus, in focusing on Thomas's role as depicted in this play, we must
conclude that the author saw him as, first, not cynically doubting the
Resurrection per se, but doubting only and specifically the resurrection
of the body; second, as concerned with ethos, but specifically with the
current state of mind of himself and his interlocutors, rather than on
his perceptions of their unchangeable character. In other words, the
concerns of this play are physicality and emotional immediacy: the
emphasis on the here and now that is key to compassion and community.

With this combination of *topoi* and this emphasis on methods of argument, the playwright is equipped with appropriate material to begin the work of *distributio*. As suggested, a combination of *logos* and *ethos* is called for, and such a combination is precisely what the play shows. When Thomas is not asserting the turbulent emotions of all those present, he and the other apostles attempt to engage each other in logical arguments which turn on the play's key *topoi*.

Some of Thomas's arguments deal wholly with the miraculous nature of the Resurrection; in these, Thomas doubts that any supernatural help can be forthcoming because Christ himself is the highest source of help and yet was killed. 'Sen he was God and ded lay,/From ded who myght hym call?' (Towneley 28/527–8). Thomas focuses on the natural processes of life that, in his mind, must govern both life and death in the absence of such miraculous aid: 'Dede has determyd his days,/Hys lyfe noght trow I may' (Towneley 28/439–40). Other arguments of Thomas focus more specifically upon the corporeality of the Resurrection, asserting, as we have seen, that the body cannot rise, only the spirit.

> When Cryst cam you to vysyte,
> As ye tell me with saw,
> A whyk man from a spyryte,
> Wherby couth ye hem knaw?   (Towneley 28/373–6)

Thus the questions of whether the Resurrection is natural or supernatural, and corporeal or noncorporeal, become key issues in the play due to Thomas's own concerns.

The Apostles' answers to Thomas's arguments are, of course, ineffective; the playwright cannot make them convince Thomas and remain true to his source. Yet several of the Apostles' answers are ineffective also from a rhetorical point of view; while they reflect orthodox dogma, they are not strictly relevant to Thomas's doubts. For instance, in reply to the first argument of Thomas quoted above, 'Quartus Apostolus' says,

> The holy gost in Marye light,
> And in hir madynhede
> Goddys Son she held and dight,
> And cled hym in manhede.
> For luf he wentt as he had hight,

To fight withoutten drede;
When he had termynd that fight,
He skypt outt of his wede.   (Towneley 28/345–52)

All of what this apostle says may be so, yet it does not answer Thomas's question, as Thomas himself points out: 'If he skypt outt of his
clethyng,/Yit thou grauntys his cors was ded' (Towneley 28/353–4).[14]
The next apostle does somewhat better, managing to assert both the
corporeality and the supernatural quality of the Resurrection:

The gost went to hell apase
Whils the cors lay slayn,
And broght the sawles from Sathanas
For which he suffred payn.
The thryd day right he gase,
Right vnto the cors agayn;
Mighty God and man he rose,
And therfor ar we fayn.   (Towneley 28/361–8)

Yet this apostle still does not really address Thomas's doubts; his asser-
tions may be true, but they are unargued. Thomas, still unconvinced,
does not even respond, asking instead for 'a skyll perfyte' (Towneley
28/371), a more definite sort of proof. Later still, he begins to ask for
what the rhetoricians call 'inartificial proof,'[15] or what modern lawyers
would call 'physical evidence':

Say, bad he any of you fele
The woundys of his body,
Flesh or bone or ilka dele,
To assay his body?   (Towneley 28/389–92)

This kind of proof takes Thomas and the Apostles fully out of the
realm of rhetoric; rhetoric 'is needed at times and in cases where the
facts don't speak for themselves,'[16] but Thomas is beginning to ask precisely for physical and eloquent facts, not for arguments from the
Apostles.

It is at this point also that Thomas breaks his previous pattern of
focusing on emotion, and begins to attack the unchanging aspects of
the *ethos* of his fellows:

> Lo, sich foly with you is,
> Wyse men that shuld be,
> That thus a womans witnes trowys
> Better then that ye se.   (Towneley 28/417–20)

The Apostles at this point are left with little recourse but to assert the truthfulness of their witnesses and the perils of Thomas's unbelief, rather than trying to argue about the doctrine itself. Ultimately, after much wrangling, Decimus Apostolus can do nothing other than to demand without proofs, 'Trow his rysyng by dayes threyn/Sen he died on the rode' (Towneley 28/555–6). Thus Thomas and his interlocutors have had to come painfully to grips with the inability of argument, logic, or speech to convey belief in the Resurrection. Ultimately, the rhetoric of the Towneley author leads the audience to the point at which argumentative rhetoric fails and faith without logical proofs must take over.

Of course, it is not a blind faith but a seeing, sensory, and compassionate faith; it is also, surprisingly, a rhetorically charged faith. At Thomas's demand at last for physical proof that he himself can experience, Christ appears and invites Thomas, 'Putt thi hande in my syde, no fres' (Towneley 28/565). Furthermore, Christ's closing speech about seeing and not seeing, while scriptural in its literal meaning, is suggestive of a more tangible, incarnational reading:

> Thomas, for thou felys me
> And my woundes bare,
> Mi risyng is trowed in the.   (Towneley 28/641–3)

The precise choice of words, 'trowed in the,' suggests not only that the Resurrection is believed *by* Thomas, but that the audience's faith in the Resurrection is to be located *in* the figure of Thomas. Such a reading is not only consistent with the Gregorian reading of Thomas which governs late medieval views of the saint, but it is also consistent with the sudden lyricism into which Thomas bursts upon seeing the risen Christ:

> Mercy, Iesu, honoure of man,
> Mercy, Iesu, mans socoure,
> Mercy, Iesu, rew thi leman;
> Mans saull thou boght full sore!

Mercy, Iesu, that may and can
Forgif syn and be socoure;
Mercy, Iesu, as thou vs wan,
Forgif and gif thi man honoure.   (Towneley 28/609–16)

This ending to Thomas's forty-eight line speech is built, like the rest of the speech, around *anaphora* on the words 'mercy, Iesu'; in addition, the *homoioteleuton* of 'forgif and gif,' the *anaphora* of 'forgif,' the *conduplicatio* of 'man[s],' and the *epanalepsis* of 'honoure of man/man honoure' knit this stanza into a web of interrelated ideas, all based upon forgiveness, grace, and human experience.

The lyricism of this speech[17] brings the play fully into a different rhetorical branch. Up until now, the play has wavered mostly between the two argumentative branches of rhetoric: judicial, in the attempts by Thomas and the Apostles to explain the facts as they understand them, and deliberative, in the Apostles' warnings to Thomas about the consequences of unbelief. Now, however, Thomas concludes the play with a strong movement into the panegyric, the rhetoric of pure praise. In its closing with the panegyric, and its intense emphasis on *pathos*, the Towneley play makes clear the equation between the physical and the pathetic that Duffy notes;[18] in its exhaustion of the logical and ethical means of persuasion, it leaves a combination of the pathetic and the physical: the primary characteristics of late medieval piety.

The Towneley play of Thomas, then, despite its faults, nonetheless has a definite doctrine and plan. An explication of the doctrines of the Resurrection, particularly its supernaturalness and corporeality, the play is also a debate whose rhetoric is precise, argumentative, progressive, and doomed to deliberate failure. Only after Thomas and the Apostles have fully explored the appropriate doctrines, only after they have argued by *logos* and by two species of *ethos*, only after they have exhausted all artificial means of discussion, does the play admit the failure of argumentative rhetoric in the arena of faith, and admit physical, panegyric, pathetic proof, located in the eloquent body of Christ itself.

In the N-Town manuscript, the episode of the Resurrection is actually split between two of the manuscript's layers of revision; each layer's effect upon an audience is therefore difficult to judge. Nonetheless, issues like those in the Towneley episode are evident. In the episode of 'Peter and John at the Sepulchre' (N-Town 36),[19] Peter and John report back to the disciples that they have found the empty tomb. Thomas responds immediately with a question that leads to speculation about whether the event is to be understood naturally or supernaturally:

> *Thomas.*   We haue grett woundyr, everychon,
>   Of þese wurdys þat ȝe do speke.
>   A ston ful hevy lay hym vpon—
>   From vndyr þat ston how xulde he breke?
> *Petrus.*   The trewth to tellyn, it passyth oure wytt!
>   Wethyr he be resyn thorwe his owyn myght,
>   Or ellys stolen out of his pitt
>   Be sum man prevely be nyght.   (N-Town 36/155–62)

This episode takes place near the end of the 'Passion Play 2' layer of the N-Town cycle,[20] which ends with Mary Magdalene's triumphant announcement to the Apostles that she has seen the risen Christ, so that Thomas's doubt goes no further. Mary Magdalene does specify that she saw Christ 'Of flesche and bon quyk levynge man' (N-Town 37/89), but the play explores the issue no more than this.

The 'N-Town pageant' episode immediately following in the manuscript is quite another case. It is marked '*Aparicio Cleophe et Luce*' (N-Town 38/s.d. 1) but contains also, as in the Chester version, the appearance to Thomas. It explores the same issues as the Towneley version, however, and in strikingly similar ways. Thomas again focuses on the emotional state of the Apostles and upon denying the corporeal and supernatural aspects of resurrection:

> Be in pes, Petyr, þu gynnyst to rave!
>   Thy wurdys be wantowne and ryght vnwyse.
> How xulde a deed man þat deed lay in grave
>   With qwyk flesche and blood to lyve ageyn ryse?   (N-Town 38/301–4)

The play does not go into the lengthy argument of the Towneley version, however, but moves quickly to Thomas's demand for physical proof (N-Town 38/321–5). It ends, however, with a long speech by Thomas, resembling the Towneley version in its rhetorical flair and panegyric effect.

> As a ravaschyd man whos witt is all gon,
>   Grett mornynge I make for my dredfful dowte.

Alas, I was dowteful þat Cryst from vndyr ston
  Be his owyn grett myght no wyse myght gone owte.
Alas, what mevyd me thus in my thought?
  My dowtefful beleve ryght sore me avexit.
The trewthe do I knowe þat God so hath wrought:
  Quod mortuus et sepultus nunc resurrexit.   (N-Town 38/353–60)

The alliteration of such phrases as 'mornynge I make' and 'dredfful dowte,' the *anaphora* on 'Alas,' the oxymoron of 'dowtefful beleve,' and the *antistasis* on 'myght' instantly transform the verse of the play from dialogue into lyric. In addition, the Latin refrain and its rhyme word, 'avexit,' occurring in five consecutive stanzas, lead the audience through a different sort of experience of the movement from doubt to faith.

In the first three stanzas of Thomas's speech, it is 'dowte' that 'avexit,' as Thomas recounts the Passion of Christ and the history of his own doubts: 'I trustyd no talys þat were me told' (N-Town 38/369). In the fourth stanza, however, the verb takes a different subject, in conjunction with a startling iconographic moment:

Thus be my grett dowte oure feyth may we preve.
  Behold my blody hand, to feyth þat me avexit;
Be syght of þis myrroure, from feyth not remeve
  Quod mortuus et sepultus nunc resurrexit.   (N-Town 38/381–4)

The play's editor glosses '*avexit*' as 'vexes, distresses' and 'harasses,'[21] but it could also mean 'conveyed to a place.' In this sudden shift of subject, this meaning seems to be in the forefront, as Thomas declares that his bloody hand has carried him over to faith. Furthermore, in one of the drama's most explicit statements of purpose, Thomas tells the audience to make of him their 'myrroure,' and affirms the Gregorian view of this episode, an affirmation that he repeats in the following stanza: 'For be my grett dowte oure feyth may we preve/Aʒens all þo eretykys þat speke of Cryst shame' (N-Town 38/387–8). In making such affirmations, Thomas is speaking in the voice of the church as a whole, rather than solely as a character in a dramatic situation. E. Catherine Dunn has argued that such a function gives the character who plays it 'a detachment from the immediate dramatic event that serves to distance the turmoil or conflict or even comic action and envelop these things in a luminous veil.'[22] Such an interpretation of either the Towneley or the N-Town play ignores the panegyric, pathetic appeal that the playwrights are so clearly attempting. It does, however, rightly suggest that the kind of speech typified by these two plays' concluding monologues goes beyond the immediate dramatic moment; indeed, in bringing both physicality and *pathos* into a moment of direct audience address, they equate the moment of Thomas's revelation with the experience of affective piety as a whole. They suggest, therefore, the terms upon which a Christian rhetoric can be based without sacrificing either eloquence or certainty.

This Christian rhetoric is most fully explored, and given perhaps its most striking mandate, in the York cycle. The York play of 'The Incredulity of Thomas' (York 41) lacks the Apostles' initial doubt, focusing instead upon their near-despair; nonetheless, the play treats the same key issues as its Towneley analogue. The issue of corporeality is central to the play:

Johannes. A *sperite* it is, þat trowe I right,
　　　All þus appered here to oure sight
　　　. . . . .
Deus.　　I ame Criste, ne drede зou noght:
　　　Her may зe se
　　　Þe same *body* þat has you bought
　　　Vppon a tre.　　　　　(York 41/37–8, 45–8, my emphasis)

The issue of natural or supernatural resurrection is of less concern; it is alluded to by Thomas, but not answered with any argument:

Thomas.　He þat was so fully slaine,
　　　Howe schulde he rise?
Jacobus.　Thomas, truly he is on lyve
　　　Þat tholede þe Jewes his flessh to riffe,
　　　He lete vs fele his woundes fyue,
　　　Oure lorde verray.　　　　　(York 41/137–42)

Nonetheless, Jacobus's immediate refusal to argue on Thomas's terms, and his quick and unsolicited report of physical evidence, imply the same conclusion that the Towneley play makes more explicit: that argument does not work; the eloquent body of Christ itself is the only possible proof. Additionally, the play ends, as it must, with the same statement by Christ that 'Blissed be they euere/ Þat trowis haly in my rising right,/ And saw it neuere' (York 41/190–2): that in the absence of physical evidence, faith must intervene.

In the York Cycle, Thomas is central to another episode, however: one in which the Virgin appears to him after her death, comforting him in his despair. This episode is unique to the York Cycle; it does not appear even in the N-Town manuscript, with its elaborate play of the death and assumption of the Virgin.[23]

The Virgin's appearance to Thomas was, nonetheless, a popularly depicted subject in the visual arts, from the first half of the fourteenth century throughout the fifteenth.[24] The legend may date from as far back as the ninth century, but its most commonly known source[25] is probably the brief account in the *Legenda aurea* that reads: 'Thomas autem cum abesset et rediens credere recusaret, subito zonam qua corpus eius precintum fuerat ab aere recipit illesam ut uel sic intellegeret totaliter fuisse assumpta' (Thomas, however, was absent [from her Assumption], and when he came back refused to believe. Then suddenly the girdle that had encircled her body fell intact into his hands, and he realized that the Blessed Virgin had really been assumed body and soul).[26] The issues surrounding the Assumption of the Virgin, and Thomas's unique experience of it, are not unlike the issues surrounding the Resurrection of Christ. Primary to the story is the issue of carnality, the claim that Mary was taken up bodily and not merely in spirit. Gibson calls the doctrine of Mary's bodily assumption 'the apotheosis of the incarnational preoccupations of the culture.'[27] Perhaps that is an exaggeration; it would seem logical that the Incarnation itself should hold such pride of place. Nonetheless there is no doubt that the doctrine of the Assumption is a crucial event in late medieval incarnational thinking, and the York play is completely in line with both the plays of the Resurrection and the popular piety of the culture in which it appeared.

Rhetorically, the play accomplishes its goal rather differently from the York cycle's play of Christ's appearance to Thomas, however. That play, as we have seen, is relatively brief, containing little argument by Thomas or the disciples, and little opportunity for non-visual proofs to be tried. The York play of the Assumption, by contrast, begins with a long monologue by Thomas, plunging the audience, at first, directly into a realm of highly wrought verbiage.

He teched full trewe, but þe tirauntes were tened.
    For he reproued þer pride þai purposed þame preste

> To mischeiue hym, with malis in þere mynde haue þei menyd,
>> And to accuse hym of cursednesse þe caitiffs has caste.
> Ther rancoure was raised, no renke might it reste,
>> Þai toke hym with treasoune, þat turtill of treuthe,
> Þai fedde hym with flappes, with fersnesse hym feste,
>> To rugge hym, to riffe hym; þer reyned no rewthe.
>> Vndewly þei demed hym:
>>> Þei dusshed hym, þei dasshed hym,
>>> Þei lusshed hym, þei lasshed hym,
>>> Þei pusshed hym, þei passhed hym,
>> All sorrowe þei saide þat it semed hym   (York 45/27–39)

Thomas's opening monologue consists of eight such stanzas, knitted together by alliteration, a complex rhyme scheme, and concatenation. The last of these is a device often signalling spiritual or emotional desperation in the York cycle; for instance, it occurs in Adam's monologue after his fall in York 6/77–122, and the two pilgrims' dialogue en route to Emmaus in York 40/1–67. Thomas also calls attention to his language itself by the use of nonsense words such as 'dusshed,' 'lusshed,' and 'passhed,' which seem to belong in this stanza for purely aural reasons.

The complexity, length, and opacity of Thomas's speech, which is little more in content than a retelling of events, can be wearying to an audience. Those who witnessed this play performed in Toronto in 1998 as part of the entire York cycle seemed irritated by it; one audience member told me that he had found Thomas infuriating, while much of the discussion on this play afterwards seemed to be centred on trying to find some other use for this monologue than a purely dramatic one.[28]

Nonetheless, if played sympathetically, Thomas's monologue may serve the same function as those of Adam and of the pilgrims to Emmaus: to portray the desperation of a pilgrim who has lost his connection with the grace that makes hope possible. It is no accident, perhaps, that Thomas is once again focusing on the death of Christ. Although he has himself been witness to the Resurrection, he is again locked into the feeling that 'My lorde and my luffe, loo, full lowe is he lapped' (York 45/3). Even his remembrance of the Resurrection gives him little comfort in itself:

To mene of his manhode my mynde was all meued.

> But þat reuerent redused me be resoune and be riȝt
>
> . . . .
>
> So sone he assendid
> Mi felaus in feere
> Ware sondered sere,
> If þai were here
> Mi myrthe were mekill amendid.   (York 45/81–8, 87–91)

In Thomas's complaint, there is more than mere loneliness; the sundering of the Apostles here may be likened to a sundering of the body of the Church. The metaphor of Church as body is made numerous times in the Pauline epistles, with such statements as, 'Sicut enim corpus unum est, et membra habet multa, omnia autem membra corporis cum sint multa, unum corpus sint: ita et Christus' (For the body is one and hath many members; and all the members of the body, whereas they are many, yet are one body: so also is Christ' [1 Cor 12: 12]), or, 'Vos autem estis corpus Christi, et membra de membro' (Now you are the body of Christ and members of member' [1 Cor 12:27]). Augustine expands the metaphor, making a crucial distinction between apostolic and post-apostolic experience:

Hoc nondum videbant discipuli: Ecclesiam per omnes gentes, incipientibus ab Jerusalem, nondum videbant. Caput videbant: et de corpore capiti credebant. Per hoc quod videbant, quod non videbant credebant. Similes illis sumus et nos: videmus aliquid, quod ipsi non videbant: et non videmus aliquid, quod ipsi videbant. Quid nos videmus, quod ipsi non videbant? Ecclesiam per omnes gentes. Quid non videmus, quod ipsi videbant? Christum in carne constitutum. Quomodo illi illam videbant, et de corpore credebant: sic nos corpus videmus, de capite credamus. Invicem nos adjuvent visa nostra. Adjuvat eos visus Christus, ut futuram Ecclesiam crederent: adjuvat nos visa Ecclesia, ut Christum resurexisse credamus.

This the disciples did not see, namely, the Church throughout all nations, beginning at Jerusalem. They saw the Head and they believed the Head in the matter of the Body. By this which they saw they believed that which they did not see. We too are like to them; we see something which they did not see, and we do not see something which they did see. What do we see which they did not? The Church throughout all nations. What is it we do not see, which they saw? Christ present in the flesh. As they saw Him and believed concerning the Body, so do we see the Body; let us believe concerning the Head. Let what we have respectively seen help us. The sight of Christ helped them to believe in the future Church; the sight of the Church helps us to believe that Christ has risen.[29]

The appearance of Mary to Thomas serves for the character the same function that the visible Church served for the faithful medieval Christian: it reinforces the understanding of Christ's resurrection and universalizes the doctrine.

When Mary first appears in this play, with a burst of angelic song, Thomas looks upon the sight, and speaks in terms that echo the sayings of Joseph and the shepherds at the Nativity:

> O glorious God what glemes are glydand,
>   I meve in my mynde what may þis bemene?
> I see a berde borne in blisse to be bidand
>   With aungelis companye, comeley and clene.   (York 45/118–21)

Tying together the Incarnation with the resurrection not only of Christ's body but also of the body of Christ's followers, Thomas moves into the same sort of panegyric mode of speech that in other contexts he uses to address the risen Christ, based this time on *anaphora* on the phrase 'I thank þe' (York 45/170–82); he then proceeds to make his way to the Apostles, as he has before. His conversation with them, however, proves the direct opposite of his conversation with the Apostles in the earlier plays. It is not Thomas but the Apostles who are in despair, and it is not the Apostles but Thomas who must supply proof.

Thomas's conversation with the Apostles brings up the same issues of proof and of the limits of verbal argument when dealing with mystery as the play of Christ's appearance, but it also reaches a rather different conclusion.

> *Petrus.*   Þat þou come not to courte here vnkyndynys þou kid vs,
>   Oure treuth has of-turned vs to tene and to trayne.
>   Þis yere hast þou rakid, þi reuth wolde not ridde vs,
>   For witte þou wele þat worthy is wente on hir waye.
>   In a depe denne dede is scho doluen þus daye,
>   Marie þat maiden and modir so milde.
> *Thomas.*   I wate wele iwis.
> *Jacobus.*   Thomas, do way.

Andreas. Itt forste noȝt to frayne hym, he will not be filde.
Thomas.   Sirs, with hir haue I spoken
            Lattar þanne yee.
Johannes. Þat may not bee.
Thomas.   Yis, knelyng on kne.
Petrus.   Þanne tite can þou telle vs some token?   (York 45/235–47)

Questioning the *ethos* of the one who brings miraculous news, regarding the passions of those who are receiving the news, the demand for
proof: all of these are the same issues that surround Christ's appearance, and Thomas resolves them in a similar way: by physical rather
than verbal proof.

Thomas. Lo þis token full tristy scho toke me to take youe.
Jacobus. A, Thomas, whare gate þou þat girdill so gode?
Thomas. Sirs, my message is meuand some mirthe for to make youe,
            For founding flesshly I fande hir till hir faire foode.
                                                        (York 45/248–51)

It may seem as if this play merely repeats the issues already addressed
by the play of Christ's appearance. Admittedly, in the York cycle the
play of Christ's appearance is quite brief, so that a revisiting of them
may not seem out of place. However, the end result of this play is quite
different from that of any play of Christ's appearance because of a key
metaphor that Thomas makes at its conclusion.

The lorde of all lordis in lande schall he lede youe
    Whillis ȝe trauell in trouble þe trewthe for to teche.
With frewte of oure feithe in firthe schall we fede youe
    For þat laboure is lufsome ilke lede for to leche.
    Nowe I passe fro youre presence þe pepull to preche,
        To lede þame and lere þame þe lawe of oure lorde.
    As I saide, vs muste asoundre and sadly enserche
        Ilke contré to kepe clene and knytte in o corde
            Off oure faithe.
                Þat frelye foode
                Þat died on rode
                With mayne and moode
He grath yowe be gydis full grath.   (York 45/300–12)

When Thomas speaks of encircling, keeping clean, knitting in one cord, he verbally equates the Apostles themselves with Mary's girdle; conversely, he suggests that Mary, in throwing down her girdle, symbolically gave him the Church.

Mary, of course, had symbolized the Church for centuries by the time of these plays,[30] and still does, but the implications in this case are quite particular. In this play is portrayed Augustine's insistence that 'adjuvat nos visa Ecclesia, ut Christum resurexisse credamus' (The sight of the Church helps us believe that Christ has risen);[31] the identification of Mary, the Apostles, the Church, and corporeal existence is subsequently what makes Christian rhetoric and persuasion – the Church's particular functions – possible. The equation is the same one that Augustine makes in saying that 'Caput vestrum peperit Maria, vos Ecclesia. Nam ipsa quoque et mater et virgo est' (Mary gave birth to your Head, the Church gives birth to you. For she also is both virgin and mother).[32] While during the Resurrection play the problem depicted was only resolvable through the direct revelation of the risen God, at this point the mission of the Church becomes clear: 'Nowe I passe fro youre presence þe pepull to preche,/To lede þame and lere þame þe lawe of oure lorde' (York 45/304–5), says Thomas. No longer is his own faith in question; he and the other Apostles now fully have the power to engage in the evangelization of others: a rhetorical act of moving the emotions of listeners in such a way as to lead them to identification with the body of the Church, with the body of Christ, and with each other.

This form of Christian rhetoric is both similar to and different from Augustine's way of dealing with the constant problems of Christian rhetoric. The Augustinian view declares that Christian rhetoric is both possible and needful, but downplays logical argument in favour of the speaker's *ethos* and the apodeictic proof of Scripture.[33] It also, as Fish argues, emphasizes its own ultimate inadequacy and the need to turn itself over to God. The plays of Thomas graphically illustrate the reasons for the lack of emphasis on logic and admit the frustration of language and reason, but also, in their various ways, point towards an incarnational kind of rhetoric: one based upon a pathetic response to the apodeictic proof of corporeality. The emphasis also upon the supernatural nature of all of the events portrayed both necessitates and reinforces that pathetic response: it is precisely the wonder of a miracle that engages Thomas, and the plays as a whole, to move into the panegyric mode, in which an audience's passions are directly engaged.

The plays of Thomas and the form of rhetoric they exemplify, then, are emblematic of the 'incarnational aesthetic'[34] of late medieval piety in general; they are also, however, instances in which the asserted certainties of faith and the intellectual dynamic of rhetoric meet and become harmonized. If they do not convince from a logical point of view, their failure to do so is made a virtue rather than a flaw: their depiction of the failure of reason in the face of miracle is replaced by direct appeal, by the visible form of Christ, and perhaps most strongly by the self-critical dramatic narrative form itself, which gains 'the demonstrative potential inherent in logical predication'[35] through its own inadequacy and the inevitable intervention of God.

3

Mary Magdalene and Ethical Decorum

The plays of Thomas not only show the limitations of argumentative rhetoric but also indicate a kind of sacramental rhetoric, one based on *pathos* and to some degree dependent on the person or *ethos* of the saint. They suggest that such a rhetoric can be an effective tool in reinforcing the audience's sense of itself as part of the sacred community of the Church – of those who believe in Christ and act accordingly. Yet at the same time, they also question the usefulness of *ethos* as a means of persuasion.

Of all the characters whose *ethos* is questioned in those plays, the most notable is Mary Magdalene, who brings the news of Christ's resurrection to the Apostles. The Digby play of *Mary Magdalene* also concentrates on the issues of *ethos* and of saintly rhetoric, but accomplishes its task differently from the Thomas plays. Recognizing that Mary Magdalene begins as one of the worldliest of sinners, the play's concern with authority and sovereignty nonetheless leads it to show her *ethos* in a favourable light by interpreting her in a way that is different from several of the traditions surrounding her legend. While such reinterpretation can lead (and has led) to modern misunderstandings of the play, it need not have confused a late medieval audience. Indeed, it is precisely by appealing to the sensibilities of a late medieval audience that the Digby *Mary Magdalene* creates a powerful character, whose *ethos* as a preacher leads to the power to realign fallen language, shifting it away from corrupt earthly authority and placing it in the service of divine and ecclesiastical authority, even as Mary Magdalene herself is transformed from a worldly (yet not inherently vicious) sinner who obeys the wrong masters to a symbol of the Church subject to Christ.

Mary Magdalene's preaching career is portrayed in terms of this conflict between worldly and holy allegiances, particularly in her encounters with the King of Marseilles. The Digby Mary Magdalene uses all the means of persuasion she can, but primary to her success is her *ethos*, including her physical appearance. The rather more than usually virtuous *ethos* of the character helps to lay the foundation for the legitimacy of her later preaching, much of which also concerns the allegiance of the minds and souls of others. While the Digby playwright does, as we shall see, stress her need for God's grace, he also strives to show her as a worthy vessel and vehicle of that grace, by establishing from the beginning an appropriately promising moral character.

'Mary Magdalene,' Helen Meredith Garth writes, 'was ranked with the Apostles by the Church and the *Acta Sanctorum* calls her [...] "the *Apostle to the Apostles.*" '[1] When the Digby playwright composed his spectacular play of the saint's life, it was central to his needs to create a character worthy of such a title. Yet his accomplishment in doing so has not always been sufficiently appreciated; in particular, his manipulation of *ethos*, *pathos*, and other rhetorical devices has largely escaped critical notice, or, when it has attracted such notice, has not received sufficient analysis.

Bowers's dismissal, for instance, of the Digby playwright's use of *decorum*[2] fails to take into account the possible dramatic functions of the high style on the medieval stage. And yet, latent in Bowers's article are the seeds of such an analysis. He is quite right to assert that the play is written largely in aureate and high diction; he is also correct in observing that the settings for Mary Magdalene's early life are upper class: not only the well-appointed tavern but also the castle in which she is first introduced to the audience. He is surely justified in noting that hagiographical writing tends to follow such patterns of *decorum*. But he does not realize that these patterns are precisely the elements that allow the audience to interpret the *ethos*, or moral character, of Mary Magdalene, and therefore the elements that are crucial to establishing Mary Magdalene as a credible and compelling orator for and before a late medieval audience.

The use of the high style theoretically implies certain characteristics both in the audience and in the speaker: the audience, it implies, is capable, culpable, and possibly unwilling; the speaker is grave, authoritative, and superior. Augustine argues, for instance, that 'Cum vero aliquid agendum est et ad eos loquimur qui hoc agere debent nec tamen volunt, tunc ea quae magna sunt dicenda sunt granditer et ad flectendos animos congruenter. [...] granditer si adversus inde animus ut convertatur impellitur' (When action must be taken and we are addressing those who ought to take it but are unwilling, then we must speak of what is important in the grand style, the style suitable for moving minds to action. [...] [One speaks] in the grand style, if antagonistic minds are being driven to change their attitude).[3] The *Rhetorica ad Herennium* notes, moreover, that the high style consists not only of impressive words but also of 'graves sententiae quae in amplificatione et commiseratione tractantur' (impressive thoughts [...] such as are used in Amplification and Appeal to Pity).[4] The use of the high style, in theory, corresponds both to the Ciceronian purpose, *movere*,[5] and to grandness of meaning and subject matter; in its impressive way it portrays a superior speaker conveying great things to a reluctant or otherwise difficult audience.

The matching of both devotional and upper-class sensibilities with the high style is not merely a literary convention for its own sake, however. Lanham writes that 'decorum as a stylistic criterion finally locates itself entirely in the beholder and not in the speech or text. No textual pattern per se is decorous or not ... Like the human visual system, rhetorical *decorum* is a bag of tricks which constitutes for us a world that it then presents as "just out there" awaiting our passive reception.'[6] This 'bag of tricks' is key to what Huizinga has called the 'need to frame emotions within fixed forms.' This need, Huizinga argues, becomes directed towards the shaping of a society based on mutual agreement of experience and unmarred by misdirected outbursts.[7]

When, therefore, the Digby playwright uses a style suited to devotional and aristocratic sensibilities, he is not violating some a priori *decorum* suited to drama, but rather signifying the nature of the society constituted by his play; he signifies also the character or *ethos* of the people who are to inhabit that society. Furthermore, he signals to the audience the response he expects them to have towards those characters. Thus, when the playwright uses the high style for Mary Magdalene, he not only portrays her as upper class, but also uses the style to create a complex web of assumptions about her behaviour, her environment, her credibility, and her possible motives: in short, her *ethos*.[8]

Thus, the legend of Mary Magdalene's prostitution must be played down. This task is difficult, given both the history of the character and the strictness of medieval English attitudes, by which any woman at variance from normative ideals might be labelled a whore.[9] Yet contrary to what many critics of the play have assumed, the Digby *Mary Magdalene* does not strongly present its heroine as a prostitute. It is true that she succumbs to worldly temptation, but her fall from grace is a result of the sins that she herself names: pride, wrath, and envy (681–3),[10] not primarily as a result of lechery or greed.

The usual picture of Mary Magdalene is well known. Susan Haskins describes it succinctly as 'a beautiful woman with long golden hair, weeping for her sins, the very incarnation of the age-old equation between feminine beauty, sexuality and sin ... the repentant prostitute who, hearing the words of Jesus Christ, repented of her sinful past and henceforth devoted her life and love to him.'[11] This picture was at least as common in the Middle Ages as it is today. It appears in medieval art, literature, and drama, and was vital to most interpretations of the saint.

Indeed, the Digby playwright has ready to hand an alternative explanation for Mary Magdalene's fall: she is weakened spiritually by her grief for the death of her father.[12] When Lechery asks Mary the reason for her grief, she replies, 'For my father I haue had grett heuynesse – /Whan I remembyr, my mynd waxit mort' (454–5).[13] It is at this moment that Lechery succeeds in coaxing Mary Magdalene out of her castle and into the tavern. Similarly, during the scene in the tavern, the gallant Corioste – who is actually Pride disguised (550) – finds it hard to appeal to Mary Magdalene's sensual nature. Upon his first attempt, he is rebuffed with the sharp, 'Why, syr, wene ӡe þat I were a kelle?' (520), and the suspicious, 'Qwat cavse þat ӡe love me so sodenly?' (523). Even upon Corioste's invitation to dance, Mary Magdalene replies surprisingly virtuously by the standards of late medieval morality: 'Syr, I asent in good maner./Go ӡe before, I sue yow nere,/ For a man at alle tymys beryt reverens' (531–3). Finally, it is not true that the dance is the moment of her fall; clearly Corioste senses that her heart is not in it, for he quickly says to her, 'Now, be my trowth, ӡe be wyth other ten' (534). It takes a further and more intoxicating delight to seduce her – 'Soppys in wynne, how love ӡe [þos]?' (536). This Mary Magdalene falls reluctantly.[14]

Nonetheless, once Mary Magdalene falls, the fall is thorough and seemingly complete. It is not, after all, a good man that she obeys in the tavern but a vice. As John Velz has argued, the issue of sovereignty and authority is of central importance in this play,[15] and the allegiance of characters, and even of language itself, plays a large part in determining the morality of their actions. For instance, when Mary Magdalene awaits her 'valentynys' in her bower (564), she specifically wishes for a lover who 'is wont to halse and kysse' her (571), echoing Flesh's earlier statement that he must 'halse and kysse' his spouse Lechery (347). She is clearly of the Flesh's party at this moment. Yet that very fact, like the allegorical nature of the vice, locates the source of Mary Magdalene's fall outside the character herself. It is not her interior *ethos*, not even her own flesh exactly, that is portrayed as corrupt, but her political and personal allegiances.

Further differences between the Digby Mary Magdalene and her analogues are apparent. Although she is presented not as a prostitute but as an upper-class lady, neither is she presented as a courtesan. Garth describes one portrayal, in which Jean Michel makes her 'a chatelaine of the fifteenth century. She sits at her dressing-table in a sumptuous boudoir, full of perfumes, flowers, and tapestries, and gives herself over to the ministrations of her two handmaidens ... They bring her her mirror, her fine liquids and her balm, and all the daintiness to keep her complexion beautiful and fresh.'[16] Yet, in the Digby play, she is not merely a high-born lady, but an inherently virtuous one: one who is worthy of being followed not only because of her station but because of her goodness.

The family of Cyrus is first introduced early in the play, at line fortynine; in their initial portrayal, they are worldly, powerful, and self-absorbed. Cyrus himself uses the kind of alliterative boast common to worldly rulers in medieval drama, and indeed, common to such characters in the Digby play as Caesar, Pilate, and Herod:

> I commav[n]d yow at onys my hestys to hold!
> Behold my person, glysteryng in gold,
>   Semely besyn of all other men!
> Cyrus is my name, be cleffys so cold!
>   I command yow all obedyent to beyn!   (52–6)

The three siblings are duly impressed by their father's power, but do not forget to give thanks to God for their prosperity. Nonetheless, the order in which they thank Cyrus and God is revealing. Lazarus says, 'Most reuerent father, I thank yow hartely ... /Now, good Lord, and hys wyll it be,/Gravnt me grace' (85, 89–90). Martha, likewise, says, 'O, ye good fathyr of grete degre ... /to se þat Lordys face/Whan ye xal hens passe!' (101, 108–9). Mary is the one sibling who thanks God first, and her worldly father second:

> Thou God of pes and pryncypall covnsell,
> More swetter is þi name þan hony be kynd!
>   We thank yow, fathyr, for your gyftys ryall,
> Owt of peynys of poverte vs to onbynd.   (93–6)

A similar contrast takes place when Cyrus dies. Both Lazarus and Martha bewail their sadness first, and only belatedly call on God for help (277–84, 291–7); Mary, however, calls on God first.

> The inwyttyssymus God þat euyr xal reyne,
>   Be hys help an sowlys sokor!
> To whom it is most nedfull to cumplayn,
>   He to bry[n]g vs owt of ower dolor;
>   He is most mytyest governowre,
> From soroyng vs to restryne.   (285–90)

Such details help to establish Mary's natural moral character, contrary to a number of expectations deriving from tradition. Wealthy and upper class, yet the least worldly of her family; tempted to worldliness, sin, and despair, yet not entirely culpable, this Mary Magdalene does not escape the sinful life of her legend but is not identified entirely with sin either.

While *ethos* is classically considered a part of the speech presently being delivered,[17] Augustine pointed out that

> Habet autem ut oboedientur audiamur quantacumque granditate dictionis maius pondus vita dicentis ... ita conversatur ut non solum sibi praemium comparet sed et praebeat aliis exemplum et sit eius quasi copia dicendi forma vivendi.

> More important than any amount of grandeur of style to those of us who seek to be listened to with obedience is the life of the speaker. [... A speaker] should seek to live in such a way that he not only gains a reward for himself but also gives an example to others, so that his way of life becomes, in a sense, an abundant source of eloquence.[18]

Or, as Gregory the Great puts it,

> Illa namque uox libentius auditorum cor penetrat, quam dicentis uita commendat, quia quod loquendo imperat, ostendo adiuuat ut fiat.

His voice penetrates the hearts of his hearers the more readily, if his way of life commends what he says. What he enjoins in words, he will help to execution by example.[19]

For a playwright giving the background history of a preaching character, then, the establishment of *ethos* from the beginning is a logical and needful technique. For a play that concerns conversion not only of an upper-class saint but of a king and queen, and that is deeply concerned with authority throughout, it is natural that the playwright should contrast Mary Magdalene's natural *ethos* with the political allegiances of the world.

During Mary Magdalene's preaching career, her *ethos*, as established from the beginning, is further developed; it also continues to be defined by factors external to her words, in addition to her sermons themselves. One of the decisive factors that establishes her *ethos* with others is her physical appearance. When Mary Magdalene's father, Cyrus, first introduces her to the audience as 'Mary, ful fayur and ful of femynyte' (71), he uses a phrase that will appear two other times. Flesh, in addressing Lechery, refers to her in similar terms: 'flowyr fayrest of femynyte' (423), and the king of Marseilles, in referring to his wife, refers to her also as 'full fayur in hyr femynyte' (943). Such expressions of beauty do not only refer to worldly women, however; long after Mary has reappeared with her companions, '*arayyd as chast women*' (s.d. 992), the Shipman's Boy refers to her as 'Nothyng butt a fayer damsell' (1412), and the Shipman himself addresses her as 'þow fayer woman' (1442). Furthermore, the king of Marseilles first refers to Mary as 'þow fayer woman' (1650) only after she has exchanged clothes with an angel; previously, he refers to her only scornfully, with such epithets as 'Thow false lordeyn' (1464). Clearly, Mary's beauty is a thread that runs throughout the play; what is not clear at first is that thread's set of implications.

Mary Magdalene's beauty has always, of course, been a byword in Christian tradition, and female beauty a dangerous and ambiguous trait. Aquinas, in fact, declared that one of the reasons why women should not preach was 'ne animi hominum aliicantur ad libidinem' (lest men's minds be enticed to lust).[20] In Bokenham's *Legendys of Hooly Wummen*,[21] however, Mary Magdalene's beauty is described both before and after her conversion, and is seen to have different effects. Before, her beauty is worldly and seductive, like that of Bathsheba or Susanna:[22]

But also þorghoute al þat regyoun
She of naturys yiftys had þe soverynte
And passyd alle wummen in excellent bewte,
For, as it semyd to yche mannes syht,
Feyrer þan she no wumman be myht.   (5390–4)

After, it is celestial but no less real in its effect:

And so greth bryhtnesse was in hir face,
That esyere yt was þe sonnys compace
In þe clerest day to beholdyn & se
Than þe bryhtnesse of hyr beute.   (6266–9)

Jacobus de Voragine, also, notes her beauty at two stages in her career, and makes particular note of the effect of her beauty upon her ability as a preacher. Jacobus writes that in her early life, Mary was famed 'quanto diuitiis et pulchritudine ... tanto corpus suum uoluptati substrauit' (for her beauty and her riches ... no less known for the way she gave her body to pleasure).[23] He also notes, however, that during her preaching career in Marseilles, 'assurgens uultu placido, facie serena, lingua diserta eos ab ydolorum cultura reuocabat et Christum constantissime predicabat. Et admirati sunt uniuersi pre specie, pre facundia, pre dulcedine eloquentie illius' (she came forward, her manner calm and her face serene, and with well-chosen words called them away from the cult of idols and preached Christ fervently to them. All who heard her were in admiration at her beauty, her eloquence, and the sweetness of her message).[24] Here, her beauty is portrayed as a rhetorical factor comparable in importance to both words and subject-matter, even when that subject matter is, explicitly, Christ. In other words, her beauty is a factor in the overall *decorum* of her preaching, and is considered a positive boon to her and to her ability as preacher, saint, and apostle. The danger of female beauty, its seductive, persuasive, or tempting capacity, is here transformed into a power for persuasion to goodness.

That a capacity for temptation can be positive is suggested rather openly at the moment of Mary Magdalene's own conversion. When the Good Angel comes to her in the garden and convinces her of her sinfulness, she bursts out:

A, how þe speryt of goodnesse hat promtyt me þis tyde,
And temtyd me wyth tytyll of trew perfythnesse!

>Alas, how betternesse in my hert doth abyde!
>   I am wonddyd wyth werkys of gret dystresse.   (602–5)

The term 'temtyd' is striking, and is emphasized by the alliteration of the line in which it appears. In *De doctrina Christiana*, Augustine repeated the Ciceronian dictum that the three goals of rhetoric were to teach, to delight, and to persuade. The states of being that these goals were to produce in the listener were, not surprisingly, that s/he was to be taught, to be pleased, and to consent.[25] 'Oportet igitur eloquentem ecclesiasticum, quando suadet aliquid quod agendum est, non solum docere ut instruat et delectare ut teneat verum etiam flectare ut vincat' (So when advocating something to be acted on the Christian orator should not only touch his listeners so as to impart instruction, and delight them so as to hold their attention, but also move them so as to conquer their minds).[26] What is somewhat striking, though by no means coincidental, is that these three goals correspond exactly with what Augustine elsewhere describes as the three states of temptation to sin. In *Sermone Domini in monte*, Augustine describes the three steps of temptation as follows: 'Nam tria sunt quibus impletur peccatum, suggestione, delectatione et consentione' (For there are three things which go to complete sin: the suggestion of it, the taking pleasure in it, and the consenting to it).[27] The parallel is unmistakable: in temptation and in rhetorical experiences in general, there come, first, awareness, second, feeling, and third, consent. The lack of any one of these elements makes the attempt at persuasion a failure; Augustine says, 'Qui ergo nititur dicendo quod bonum est, nihil illorum trium spernens – ut scilicet doceat, ut delectet, ut flectat' (So the speaker who is endeavouring to give conviction to something that is good should despise none of these three aims – of instructing, delighting, and moving).[28] Furthermore, the presence of these parallel triads in both a work on rhetoric and a description of psychological faculties suggests that Augustine saw a similarity between the structure of persuasion and the structure of a human being.

There is a difference, however, in the particular causes of each stage of persuasion, depending on whether the final object be sin or doctrine. In the case of sin, Augustine identifies the causes of the stage of awareness as being either memory or the bodily senses, stimulated 'lubrico et volubili, hoc est, temporali corporum motu' (by a fleeting and rapid, i.e., a temporary, movement of bodies).[29] In contrast, the same stage in the case of doctrine 'in rebus est constituta quas dicimus' (resides in the subject-matter of our discourse),[30] in other words, in the raw subject matter of Scripture and the exposition thereof. Similarly, the cause of delight in the case of sin is said to be 'in appetitu autem carnali' (the carnal appetite),[31] while in the case of doctrine it is a rational response to eloquence in speech and in logic.[32] Finally, the cause of consent in the case of sin is the reason's submission to the carnal appetite,[33] while in the case of doctrine it is the reason's consent to the speech that it hears.[34] The chief difference, it will appear, is that the learning of true doctrine is basically a rational response in all three stages, while temptation to sin is the subordination of reason to animal urges. Again, the difference between goodness and sin lies largely in the direction of one's obedience.

Although Mary Magdalene's preaching career might be said properly to begin with her announcement of the empty tomb to the Apostles, the main event of legend is her conversion of the king of Marseilles. The paganism of Marseilles, as depicted by the Digby playwright, is a distorted mirror of the kind of Christianity familiar to a late medieval English audience; but it is nonetheless paganism and idolatry, a system of empty signs. Augustine, in *De doctrina Christiana*, makes the following distinction between signifier and signified, as well as his conclusions on the interpretive importance of *caritas*:

Sub signo enim servit qui operatur aut veneratur aliquam rem significantem, nesciens quid significet ... Qui autem non intellegit quid significet signum et tamen signum esse intelleget nec ipso premitur servitute ... Huic autem observationi ... cavemus figuratam locutionem, id est translatem, quasi propriam sequi ... quidquid in sermone divino neque ad morumhonestatem neque ad fidei veritatem proprie referri potest figuratum esse cognoscoas. Morum honestas ad diligendum deum et proximum ... Non autem praecipit scriptura nisi caritatem, nec culpat nisi cupiditatem ... Caritatem voco motum animi ad fruendum deo propter ipsum et se atque proximo propter deum; cupiditatem autem motum animi ad fruendum se et proximo et quolibet corpore non propter deum.

A person enslaved by a sign is one who worships some thing which is meaningful but remains unaware of its meaning ... The person who does not understand what a sign means, but at least understands that it is a sign, is not himself subject to slavery ... [T]his rule ... warns us not to pursue a figurative (that is, metaphorical) expression as if it were literal ... [A]nything in the divine discourse that cannot be related either to good morals or to the true faith should be taken as figurative. Good morals have to do with our love of God and our neighbour ... [S]cripture enjoins nothing but love [*caritas*], and censures nothing but lust [*cupiditas*] ... By love I mean the impulse of one's mind to enjoy God on his own account and to enjoy oneself and one's neighbour on account of God, and by lust I mean the impulse of one's mind to enjoy oneself and one's neighbour and any corporeal thing not on account of God.[35]

Throughout the course of the conversion of the king of Marseilles, Mary Magdalene labours to replace a set of empty signifiers with a set of meaningful ones. But in addition to this effort, the character is used to reinforce the audience's faith in that matrix of signs within which the audience itself lives, namely that of late medieval Christianity, by reinforcing the importance not just of the signifiers, but of their connection to the sovereignty of the true God. Calling primarily upon Mary Magdalene's established *ethos*, the Digby playwright makes his heroine the emblem and spokeswoman for the medieval Christian system even as she destroys the pagan parody of it.

Differences between the Christian and pagan worlds are manifold; one key difference, however, lies in their different ways of using signifiers. In particular, the Christian world is seen to subordinate even spectacularly visual signifiers to the transparency of language, while the pagan world reduces even language to the opaque. For instance, Pentecost, the emblem of linguistic understanding but also a potentially spectacular visual display, is not portrayed visually; rather, it occurs offstage while 'þe Kyng of Marcyll xall begynne a sacryfyce' (s.d. 1132). The event is recalled verbally, however, by Mary Magdalene herself. Entering 'wyth hyr dysypull' (s.d. 1335), she says,

A, now I remembyr my Lord þat put was to ded
    Wyth þe Jewys, wythowttyn gyltt or treson!
Þe therd nygth he ros be þe myth of hys Godhed;
    Vpon þe Sonday had hys gloryus resurrexcyon,
    And now is þe tyme past of hys gloryus asencyon;
He steyyd to hevyn, and þer he is kyng.
    A! Hys grett kendnesse may natt fro my mencyon!
Of alle maner tonggys he ʒaf vs knowyng,

For to vndyrstond every langwage.
Now have þe dysypyllys take þer passage

> To dyvers contreys her and ʒondyr,
> To prech and teche of hys hye damage –
> Full ferr ar my brothryn departyd asondyr.   (1336–48)

Pentecost is here rendered entirely verbal; rather than a spectacle seen by the audience, it is able to be portrayed only through words.

By contrast, the system of paganism depicted in the play renders words opaque, able to signify merely as distorted, parodic icons of the true church rather than as symbols of anything transcendent. While the gift of tongues is being given to the Apostles, the king of Marseilles participates in a ceremony that centres upon the antithesis of language: a liturgy of mock Latin and meaningless sound:

> *Leccyo mahowndys, viri fortissimi sarasenorum:*
> *Glabriosum ad glvmandum glvmardinorum,*
> *Gormondorum alcorum, stampatinatum cursorum,*
> *Cownthtys fulcatum, congrvryandum tersorum.*   (1186–9)

The mock liturgy, with its opening line of (more or less) actual Latin and its repeated use of Latinate forms such as the genitive plural suffix, cannot but serve as a kind of parody. It is also largely composed of what can only be called barbarisms. In the Digby *Mary Magdalene*, this contrast between opacity, of calling attention to language for its own sake, and clarity, of declaring language to be a rhetorical vehicle for divine authority, frames the conflict between paganism and Christianity in the court of Marseilles.

The words of paganism, directed as they are to an idol, may seem efficacious to those who live within their matrix; yet to the Christian audience, whatever rhetorical ornamentation they may have is merely empty decoration. For example, there is the king's own prayer to his idol:

> *Rex dicitt.* Mahownd, þou art of mytys most,
> In my syth a gloryus gost –
> Þou comfortyst me both in contre and cost,
>   Wyth þi wesdom and þi wytt,
>   For truly, lord, in þe is my trost.
>   Good lord, lett natt my sowle be lost!
>   All my cownsell well þou wotst,
>   Here in þi presens as I sett.   (1210–17)

Were it not for the first word of this speech, it might easily be mistaken for a pious and acceptable prayer from a virtuous character; nonetheless, it is clearly directed to the wrong lord. As John Velz puts it, 'grace and morality are a matter of being subject to the right king.'[36] When it is directed to the wrong king, even its rhetorical ornamentation, such as its alliteration, becomes mere decoration, as empty as the King's own finery of costume. Furthermore, when directed to the wrong king, sacramental signifiers such as the relic of 'Mahowndys own yeelyd!' (1237) function in a manner that is the precise opposite of that of Christian sacraments:

> 3e may have of þis grett store;
> And ye knew þe cavse wherfor,
> Ytt woll make yow blynd for ewyrmore,
>   Þis same holy bede!   (1238–41)

They are not only ineffective, but also counterproductive.

The audience is thus placed into a position radically outside the world of Marseilles. Able to recognize the intended functions of the pagan signifiers, they nonetheless are able to see their emptiness. This world, they can see, is not like theirs. They then are able to view with understanding of both form and function the result when Mary Magdalene enters the world of the pagan system and begins to challenge that system by argument and *ethos*, signified once again by differences in style as well as in matter.

It is notable that, in this version of the story, Mary Magdalene does not set out for Marseilles for the reason usual to her story. In the *Legenda aurea* and in such subsequent retellings as the *South English Legendary*,[37] Mary Magdalene and several other disciples 'ab infidelibus impositi et pelago sine aliquo gubernatore expositi ut omnes scilicet submergerentur diuino tandem nutu Marsiliam aduenerunt' (were herded by the unbelievers into a ship without pilot or rudder and sent out to sea so that they might all be drowned, but by God's will they eventually landed at Marseilles).[38] In the Digby *Mary Magdalene*, however, there is nothing accidental about either Mary's journey or her vocation as preacher.

> [*Jhesus*.] Raphaell , myn angell in my syte,
> To Mary Mavdleyn decende in a whyle,
>   Byd here passe þe se be my myth,

And sey she xall converte þe land of Marcyll.

. . . .

[*Angelus.*] Abasse þe novtt, Mary, in þis place!
Ower Lordys preceptt þou must fullfyll.
  To passe þe see in shortt space,
Onto þe lond of Marcyll.

Kyng and quene converte xall ȝe,
  And byn amyttyd as an holy apostylesse.

. . . .

[*Mari Mawdleyn.*] With þi grace, good Lord in Deite,
  Now to þe see I wyll me hy,
  Sum sheppyng to asspy.   (1368–71, 1376–81, 1390–2)

This deliberate, not accidental, undertaking to the king, not merely the
people at random, identifies Mary Magdalene's oratory as central to
her sainthood. Indeed, even the character's traditional role as weeper
at the foot of the cross is transformed into pure oratory, when, as one of
the three Marys, she enters to recall the crucifixion verbally to an audience that has not, in this play, actually seen it (993–1022). As a result,
when Mary Magdalene embarks upon her preaching career, her character as a whole reaches its most fully developed; calling fully upon
the power of her *ethos* the playwright presents a compelling character
who acts as mediator, intercessor, and above all as preacher.

Mary's initial appearance before the king of Marseilles is not, as in
the *Legenda aurea*, in reaction to any specific act of sacrifice, but more
generally 'Of my Lordys lawys to she[w] þe sentens,/Bothe of hys
Godhed and of hys powere' (1452–3). After a brief altercation with the
king, who demands to know of the power of her God, she repeats the
Genesis 1 account of creation (1481–1525), with one major difference:
her quotation of the 'in principio' of the Gospel according to John
rather than that of Genesis:

Syr, I wyll declare al and sum,
  What from God fyrst ded procede.
He seyd, '*In principio erat verbum.*'
  And wyth þat he provyd hys grett Godhed!   (1481–4)

In stressing the importance of the transcendent and transparent Word,
Mary Magdalene challenges the pagan system at its root. She also uses

a subdued style rather than a grand one, echoing Augustine's insistence that an orator 'Persuadet autem in summisso genere vera esse quae dicit' (in the restrained style [...] persuades people that what he says is true).[39] In other words, the orator teaches using that style. The king's reply explicitly reveals the nature of his paganism and of Mary Magdalene's task as rhetor:

> Herke, woman, thow hast many resonnys grett!
>   I thyngk, onto my goddys aperteynyng þey beth!
> But þou make me answer son, I xall þe frett,
>   And cut þe tong owt of þi hed!   (1526–9)

The king's challenge is surprisingly detailed in its implications. In noting Mary Magdalene's 'many resonnys grett,' he can only be referring to the facts of the creation story she has just told. With his second line, however, the king reinterprets their function as that of rhetorical commonplaces; rather than evidence specifically leading to the worship of her God, he implies that they can also be applied equally well to another goal or conclusion. In his view, conditioned by his system, words are not transparent to a clear meaning, but rather are opaque instruments capable of direction to numerous targets.

Furthermore, his threat to cut out Mary Magdalene's tongue suggests not only a personal discomfort with her words, but also his pagan religion's inability with words in general. Appropriately, in answering Mary Magdalene's challenge, the king responds not with his own words but with visual icons:

> Hens to þe tempyll þat we ware,
>   And þer xall thow se a solom syth.
> Com on all, both lesse and more,
>   Thys day to se my goddys myth!   (1534–7)

Upon their arrival at the temple, however, the king's demand of words from his idol leads to the downfall, both figurative and literal, of his idol and its priesthood:

> Lord, I besech þi grett myth,
>   Speke to þis Chrisetyn þat here sestt þou!
>   Speke, god lord, speke! Se how I do bow!
> Herke, þou pryst! Qwat menytt all this?

What? Speke, good lord, speke! What eylytt þe now?
Speke, as thow artt bote of all blysse!   (1540–5)

Upon the failure of the idol to utter a word, Mary Magdalene utters the first genuine Latin in the temple, with literally spectacular results.

The replacement of mock Latin with real Latin, of mere form with actual language, of warped icon with transparent sign, leads to the downfall of the entire pagan system.

Mary. Dominus, illuminacio mea, quem timebo?
Dominus, protecctor vite mee, a quo trepedabo?

Here xal þe mament tremyll and quake.

. . . .
Here xall comme a clowd from heven, and sett þe tempyl on afyer, and þe pryst and þe cler[k] xall synke.   (1552–s.d.1553, s.d. 1561)

In sum, what has happened here is a pair of stylistic realignments. The first is the revelation that the 'mament' is merely an empty sign, and along with it the liturgy, the prayer of the king, the relics, the temple, the whole pagan system. The second is the removal of the parodic signifiers of the Christian system, so that the Christian system itself can take root in the world of the court of Marseilles.[40]

Replacing the visible signs of the temple, however, are not only the verbal prowess of the preacher, but a set of visual signs centred on the *ethos* of the preacher. In particular, the white mantle that Mary Magdalene dons is crucial to her success.[41]

[*2nd Angel.*] In a mentyll of white xall be ower araye.
    The dorys xall opyn aȝens vs be ryth.
Mary. O gracyus God, now I vndyrstond!
    Thys clothyng of whyte is tokenyng of mekenesse.   (1604–7)

This 'tokenyng' seems intended only for the king's dreaming state, not for his waking, since immediately after Mary Magdalene speaks to the sleeping king she 'woydyt, and þe angyll and Mary chongg hyr clotheyng' (s.d. 1617), apparently back to her ordinary costume. The effect of her symbolic clothing, however, opens up the possibility of the king's conversion:

[*Rex.*] A fayer woman I saw in my syth,
All in whyte was she cladd;
  Led she was wyth an angyll bryth,
To me she spake wyth wordys sad.   (1622–5)

Yet as the sequence of the king's memories seems to indicate, he is to move from the opaque to the transparent in his understanding. The divine court to which the king is to devote himself uses all the rhetorical means at its disposal (emphasising the word more than the visual, but not lacking the visual), but the efficacy of those means is determined by the correctness of the court's hierarchy; in the realm of human action, that correctness is manifest as the allegiance of the soul.

Appropriately, when the king speaks next with Mary Magdalene, he may address her as 'Thow fayer woman' (1650), but more importantly he asks her to 'reherse here presentt,/The joyys of yower Lord in heven' (1656–7). The moment of the king's actual conversion, however, may be said to follow the queen's discovery of her miraculous pregnancy, with the following exchange:

Rex. Now, fayer womman, sey me þe sentens,
I beseche þe, whatt is þi name?
Mary. Syr, aȝens þat I make no resystens!
Mary Mavdleyn, wythowtyn blame.   (1672–5)

The King's address of Mary Magdalene again refers to her appearance, but his interest is in the meaning or 'sentens' of her name. Her reply, 'Mary Mavdleyn, wythowtyn blame,' does not reflect a mere metrical tag as it may seem to do; rather, it refers directly to one given etymology of her name as given in the *Legenda aurea*: 'Magdalena dicitur quasi manens rea' (Mary is called Magdalene, which is understood to mean 'remaining guilty').[42] Furthermore, her following demand that the king 'xall thankytt Petyr, my mastyr, wythowt delay' (1680), thus sending him across the sea on the journey that leads apparently to his wife's death, seems to refer to yet another etymological meaning of her name: 'Maria interpretatur amarum mare' (The name Mary, or Maria, is interpreted as [...] bitter sea).[43] The empty visual signs of the pagan world have vanished, replaced by words that are transparent to significance; the sovereignty of the King is placed under the sovereignty of the Church and its saints.

The arrival of the king at Jerusalem makes complete the replacement of pagan *res* with Christian *signa*, with the focus still upon the signified, or *sentens*. The king's conversation with Peter exemplifies this change.

> *Rex.* A, holy fathyr, how my hart wyll be sor
>   Of cummav[n]ddementt, and ʒe declare nat þe sentens!
> *Petyr.* Syr, dayly ʒe xall lobor more and more,
>   Tyll þat ʒe have very experyens.
>   Wyth me xall ʒe wall to have more eloquens,
> And goo vesyte þe stacyons, by and by;
>   To Nazareth and Bedlem, goo wyth delygens,
> And be yower own inspeccyon, yower feyth to edyfy.
>
> *Rex.* Now, holy father, derevorthy and dere,
>   Myn intent now know ʒe.
> It is gon full to ʒere
>   Þat I cam to yow owere þe se.   (1843–54)

Several aspects of this conversation demonstrate the key points that the playwright is making about Christian symbolism, rhetoric, and experience.

The first of these points is Peter's insistence that Christian eloquence is the product of 'very experyens' brought on by the triggers of collective and affective memory: his explanation that the king must 'wall,' or go on pilgrimage, to gain eloquence, asserts the nostalgic power of 'þe stacyons' and their ability to bring knowledge through the pure 'inspeccyon' of the pilgrim. The second point stems from the fact that the king at this time is already converted. Although Mary Magdalene's power to convert has been demonstrated, the eloquence the king is to cultivate is not itself for that purpose. George A. Kennedy observes that, at the most basic level, 'Augustine [...] regarded conversion as an act of the Spirit in which eloquence has no true role. [...] The function of Christian eloquence in Augustine's system is to convert belief into works, to impel the faithful to the Christian life.'[44] Appropriately, the king has already been baptized (1840) when he undertakes his journey, his 'feyth to edyfy' (1850). The third point that the playwright makes is that faith is based closely upon personal experience, once one has submitted to the proper authority. This point is made the more graphic by the fact that Peter, the first pope, sends the king to have 'very experyens' rather than preaching to him. It is not the case either, however, that the king's experience is to occur independently; Peter intends, so he says, to accompany the king on his pilgrimage. Thus the playwright uses this episode to suggest to the audience that the Christian soul is impelled to the Christian life by a guided journey under the proper authority of the Church, whose function it is to help the faithful achieve a personal experience of the truth.

The final emphasis upon the importance of the individual experience is that the king's own experience is not portrayed. Within a few lines, the king declares two years to be over and his journey to be complete. This strange piece of staging (or of non-staging) may reflect some of the transiency of affective mystical experience,[45] but more likely it reflects the ineffably personal quality of that experience. The playwright may be willing to lead the audience through its own 'wall to have more eloquens,' but he is not willing to portray the inner workings of another's experience.

This point is rendered sharper when one examines the audience's own trip through the 'stacyons,' led by Mary Magdalene. During the king of Marseille's first appearance (925–62), the Crucifixion happens out of sight of the audience, to be recounted verbally by 'þe thre Mariis arayyd as chast women, wyth sygnis of þe passyon pryntyd ypon þer brest' (s.d. 992):

> [*Mawdleyn.*] Alas, alas, for þat ryall bem!
>   A, þis percytt my hartt worst of all!
> For *here* he turnyd aȝen to þe woman of Jerusalem,
>   And for wherynesse lett þe crosse falle!
> *Mary Jacobe.* Thys sorow is beytterare þan ony galle,
> For *here* þe Jevys spornyd hym to make hym goo.   (993–8, my emphasis)

The events marked by the two occurrences of 'here' seem to correspond, in modern Catholic devotion, to the eighth and ninth stations of the cross, in which Jesus speaks to the women of Jerusalem, and falls for the third time, respectively.[46] The leading of communal response seems perhaps to be within the playwright's mandate, as in the stage direction following the raising of Lazarus, 'Here all þe pepull and þe Jewys, Mari and Martha, wyth on voys sey þes wordys: "We beleve in yow, Savyowr, Jhesus, Jhesus, Jhesus!"' (s.d. 920), although it seems on the whole unlikely that this brief shout was meant for the audience to join in. The characters' response to the Passion, however, such as one finds in the N-Town passion sequence, is not portrayed; rather, it is cued rhetorically in the audience by the three Maries. The audience's response is to be its own.

This is not the only moment when such rhetorical and affective emphasis occurs. Previously, the crucifixion has also taken place 'off-stage,' while the king of Marseilles introduces himself and the devil takes his leave (925–92); following this incident, Mary Magdalene, Mary Jacobe, and Mary Salome also guide the audience through a purely rhetorical and retrospective experience of the event. In this passage, the three Maries establish the presence and location of holy places in a manner not unlike the memorial techniques of antiquity and of medieval rhetorical education. The difference is that, instead of locating memories within a purely imaginary landscape, they locate them within the actual landscape of the playing space.[47] While there is nothing for the audience to see except for the Maries themselves, their words create ritual space without the need for architectural signs. The persons of the Maries, the signs of the passion they wear, and their words are sufficient.

When the king of Marseilles, then, visits Peter with the intent to 'vesyte þe stacyons, by and by' (1848), it is no wonder that his experience remains unportrayed; nor is it surprising that the queen's experience is not only unportrayed but also uncanny:

[*Regina.*] O demvr Mavdlyn, my bodyys sustynavns!
　Þou hast wr[a]ppyd vs in wele from all waryawns,
And led me wyth my lord i[n]to þe Holy Lond!
　I am baptysyd, as ye are, be Maryvs gyddavns,
Of Sent Petyrys holy hand.

I sye þe blyssyd crosse þat Cryst shed on hys precyvs blod;
　Hys blyssyd sepulcur also se I.
Whe[r]for, good hosbond, be mery in mode,
　For I have gon þe stacyounys, by and by!　　　　　(1902–10)

Though the Queen may have gone the stations indeed, the audience is not privileged to see her do so; rather, their perspective is, once again, purely rhetorical and imaginative.

In all of these events, the figure of Mary Magdalene has functioned as mediator, allowing both the other characters and the audience to interpret their experiences in such a way as to encourage the faith she symbolizes. In the example of the king and queen of Marseilles, as we have seen, her mediation is direct. It is also acknowledged, as when the queen credits Mary Magdalene for saving her life and leading her, as it were, through the stations.[48] The final episodes of Mary Magdalene's life, those that take place in the desert, are portrayed in a rather different way, one that throws the queen's closed-off experience open to the audience, and that brings the possibility of such experience into the present.

The *Legenda aurea* says little to introduce this period of the saint's life, saying merely that 'Interea beata Maria Magdalena superne contemplationis auida asperrimam heremum petiit et in loco angelicis manibus preparato per xxx annos incognita mansit' (At this time blessed Mary Magdalene, wishing to devote herself to heavenly contemplation, retired to an empty wilderness, and lived unknown for thirty years in a place made ready by the hands of angels).[49] In the Digby play, Mary Magdalene herself says little more, but what she does say is revealing.

> In þis deserte abydyn wyll wee,
>   My sowle from synne for to save;
> I wyll evyr abyte me wyth humelyte,
>   And put me in pacyens, my Lord for to love.   (1989–92)

It is striking that Mary uses the plural pronoun, seemingly including the audience in her hermitage. If the audience was not permitted to view or participate in the experience of the king and queen, they are explicitly allowed to be part of that of the saint.

> And ferdarmore, I wyll leven in charyte,
>   At þe reverens of Ower Blyssyd Lady,
>   In goodnesse to be lyberall, my sowle to edyfye.   (1997–9)

Here, again, the saint drops a striking detail, namely, the reference to the Virgin Mary. Throughout the end of the Marseilles episode, the play has shown a curious tendency to conflate its central character with the Virgin; it goes so far as to show the king addressing Mary Magdalene thus:

> Heyll be þou, Mary! Ower Lord is wyth the!
>   The helth of ower sowllys, and repast contemplatyff!
> Heyll, tabyrnakyll of þe blyssyd Trenite!
>   Heyll, covnfortabyll sokore for man and wyff!   (1939–42)

In this final episode, the saint's conflation with the Virgin becomes rather more complex. Though she explicitly states that she will live at the Virgin's 'reverens,' thus betokening a separation of identity, she nonetheless will remind audiences strikingly of her namesake, particularly in her assumption into Heaven at the end.

This similarity may be rendered the more striking depending on how she is costumed during this scene. Iconographically, Mary Magdalene in the desert is often depicted nude, clothed only in her long, all-covering hair. Yet Clifford Davidson points to one early fifteenth-century example which depicts her instead wearing 'a blue mantle over her kirtle';[50] if a costume like this was used, then her similarity to the Virgin may have been both evident and striking.[51] There is, however, no sure way of knowing how Mary Magdalene is supposed to be clothed.

At any rate, her function in the final scenes of the play is dual: both saint and layperson, she acts in relation to God and to the 'holy prest in þe same wyldyrnesse' (s.d. 2038). Both of these relationships, in turn, act to strengthen the audience in community and in faith by establishing a *decorum* reflective not of earthly but of heavenly status: a *decorum* of, in fact, the Church and its faithful. Ultimately, her task in these final scenes is to leave the earth behind – not for her own sake, but as a way of turning her functions over to the Church and its people who remain on earth: particularly the members of the Church who are present as the audience.

When Mary Magdalene partakes of the sacrament 'in nubibus' (s.d. 2030), her words are echoed by the Priest who appears below her; furthermore, both of their speeches echo the words of Jesus spoken a few lines before. The resulting knitting together of thought and word suggests a single frame of reference common to all three.

[*Jhesus.*] *Wyth joy of angyllys,* þis lett hur receyve.
   Byd hur injoye wyth all hur afyawns,
For fynddys *frawd xall hur non deseyve.*

. . . .

[*Mari.*] *O þou Lord of lorddys,* of hye domenacyon!
   In hewen and erth worsheppyd be *þi name.*
How þou devydyst me from hovngure and wexacyon!
   O gloryus Lord, *in þe is no fravddys* nor no defame!
   But I xuld serve my Lord, I were to blame,
Wych fullfyllyt me *wyth so gret felicite,*

Wyth melody of angyllys shewit me gle and game,
And have fed me wyth fode of most delycyte!

Her xall speke an holy prest in þe same wyldyrnesse, þus seyyng þe prest:

[*Prest.*] O lord of lorddys! What may þis be?
    So gret mesteryys shewyd from heven,
Wyth grett myrth and melody
    Wyth angyllys brygth as þe lewyn!
    Lord Jhesu, for *þi namys* sewynne,
    As gravnt me grace þat person to se!   (2008–10, 2039–44)

In the above citation, the words and phrases that repeat in some variation between the three speakers are italicized; the *anaphora* of 'Wyth,' the *diacope* of 'lord/lorddys,' and the *epimome* of several phrases knit the stanzas together through repetition. Between them, one can see the important points of the society of faith that they form: Jesus as Lord of lords, the importance of his name or names, the devil's fraud and Jesus' lack of it, and the joy and melody of angels.

The way that the three characters interact on stage brings this society of faith into focus. The *ethos* of Mary Magdalene continues to be emphasized. The other characters refer to her as 'wel-belovyd frynd' (2004), as one who cannot be deceived by 'fyndyys frawd' (2010), as 'Crystys delecceon' (2045), 'swetter þan sugur or cypresse' (2046),[52] 'Grett [...] wyth God for þi perfythnesse' (2048), and many another epithet of praise. Furthermore, her own actions continue to show her virtue not only in piety but in courtesy, as when she tells the priest,

[Þ]ou art wolcum onto my syth,
    Yf þou be of good conversacyon.
As I thynk in my delyth,
    Thow sholddyst be a man of devocyon.   (2061–4)

But while the importance of *ethos* remains as strong in this section as in the conversion scenes in Marseilles, it is not the conversion of characters but the reinforcement of the community of faith that is its explicit as well as implicit function.

This community of faith, constituted on stage by the three characters just mentioned, undergoes a rapid expansion as the play draws to its end. During the thirty years of Mary Magdalene's hermitage, she has received the Host from God in Heaven; just before her death, however, she is to receive it from the earthly priest. Their words together show the degree to which the saint is disengaging from earthly life:

[*Presbityr*.] Þou blyssyd woman, invre in mekenesse,
   I have browth þe þe bred of lyf to þi syth,
To make þe suere from all dystresse,
   Þi sowle to bryng to euyrlastyng lyth.
Mari. O þou mythty Lord of hye mageste,
   Þis celestyall bred for to determyn,
Thys tyme to reseyve it in me,
   My sowle þerwyth to illumyn.   (2101–8)

Furthermore, the priest's final words in the play show the degree to which the community of faith suddenly widens to include the audience as a whole:

Pryst. Now, frendys, thus endyt thys matere –
   To blysse bryng þo þat byn here!
   Now, clerkys, wyth woycys cler,
     'Te Deum lavdamus' lett vs syng!   (2136–9)

In calling for a canticle to end the play, the Digby playwright attempts to move the audience to act as one in faith; by making the character of the priest do so, to the accompaniment of the procession of the saint's body, he emphasizes the sacramental function of his central figure and of her story. Finally, by bringing the audience into the play as part of the final procession, the Digby playwright connects them bodily with the entirety of the Church of history; the audience's role is to be the same sacred community that the play has just evoked.

Ultimately, the Digby playwright acknowledges that the power of God alone can bring his audience to eternal bliss; yet in linking that acknowledgment with a well known hymn, a procession, and an awareness of the audience's presence through direct address, he incorporates the audience fully into the 'matere' of which he writes: 'Now, frendys, thus endyt thys matere – /To blysse bryng þo þat byn here!' (2136–7). Though he has emphasized the importance of the character of Mary Magdalene throughout the action of the play, in the end he turns her function over to that of the Church as a whole: it is what must sustain and nurture faith and the faithful. As Clifford Davidson has noted, however, Mary Magdalene 'was closely associated with the idea of the Church itself. As such, she was seen as an exemplar of the Christian life in its ideal form, providing a pattern for all to follow in movement from a fallen state to penitence and then to carefully introspective contemplation. [...] [H]ence her character may in the end be said to encompass the members of the audience as the action of the play, performed on the East Anglian place-and-scaffold stage, may in turn have seemed physically to encompass them.'[53] It has been argued that the only link among the multifarious parts of this play is the character of Mary Magdalene herself.[54] Yet the importance that the playwright places upon her *ethos* combined with her sacramental function as saint makes this no mere thread of commonality. Rather, her omnipresence is a constant reminder to the audience of the Christian life, of the Church, and of their own role within the Church. An audience judges *ethos* by its own view of the good life;[55] conversely, it also is given the chance to see and reinforce its view of the good life by observing a compelling exemplar of it. In the creation of his Mary Magdalene, not a repentant whore of another land, but a noble, eloquent, and ethical preacher, exemplar, and sacramental power in the context of late medieval Christianity, the Digby playwright gives his audience not only a figure to admire, imitate, and follow, but also a bridge between themselves and the Church of the Apostles.

4

Joseph, Pathos, and the Audience

The *ethos* of Mary Magdalene and the power of her rhetoric, as we have seen, are effective tools in realigning both language and the sympathies of the audience to a position of faith and community. Just as the East Anglian audience of the Digby plays is asked to take the final step in imagining and effecting the process of salvation in themselves, so also the audience of the York Cycle must enter into the world of the play and of salvation history; they are asked to do so through sympathy, and the York Cycle helps them to do so in a number of ways. One of the most vivid and memorable ways is through the character of Joseph, the foster-father of Christ. In the arc of his story, Joseph moves from a position of doubt to a position of faith, but he also moves increasingly closer to the motives and interests of the audience. From the beginning depicted as an ordinary man, Joseph by the end of his story appears also as one who is fully able, both despite his human frailty and because of it, to be called a saint and an example of holiness for the audience.

The York Cycle's portrayal of Joseph is among the most complex, and certainly among the most varied, in all of Middle English drama. Much of this character's singularity stems from his unusual textual history; like the Virgin, he plays a key role in the Gospels though they provide few details about him; like her, he was the subject of much apocryphal writing; unlike her, his cult was just coming into its own when the Middle English drama was developing. These three strands of writings on Joseph combine to form a somewhat problematic character for a playwright who intends to convey an orthodox point of view to an audience, and to move them to a position of faith.

The elements that these strands contributed to the plays are reasonably simple to identify. Joseph plays a role in only two of the four canonical Gospels: Matthew and Luke. In Matthew, angels visit Joseph to assure him of Mary's virginity (Matthew 1:20–1), to warn him to flee with Christ to Egypt (Matthew 2:13), and to advise him to return with Christ to Nazareth (Matthew 2:20). Joseph says not a word in response, but follows instructions and vanishes, his role as plot device fulfilled. In Luke, his role is even humbler. The angels in this account visit Mary and a group of shepherds, but they do not visit Joseph (Luke 1:26–38; 2:8–14). In addition, Christ's first reported words in Luke are, 'Quid est quod me quaerebatis? nesciebatis quia in his quae Patris mei sunt, oportet me esse?' (How is it that you sought me? did you not know, that I must be about my Father's business? [Luke 2:49]). And with that statement of disowning, Joseph drops out of the Gospels.

The apocryphal sources are far more detailed, and were highly influential upon medieval art and drama.[1] Marina Warner notes that the 'religious dramas followed the *Book of James'* [or *Protevangelium*] account,'[2] yet that was far from the only apocryphal gospel that shows influence upon the drama. Another source, and a slightly more acceptable one from an ecclesiastical point of view, was the *Gospel of Pseudo-Matthew*, which was in fact compiled in order to present the crude and widely condemned (but extremely popular) material of the *Protevangelium* in a more acceptable form.[3] Finally, there is the short *Gospel of the Nativity of Mary*, which in its relative restraint may have appealed to the more doctrinally conscious of the playwrights.

The *Protevangelium* introduces the elderly Joseph of medieval art, and the cranky, comical Joseph of the cycle plays. It tells at length of his troubles about Mary, and provides a detailed account: Joseph is in another town for the first months, so that the sight of Mary's pregnant body catches him by surprise. He 'smote his face, and threw himself upon the ground on sackcloth, and wept bitterly, saying, [...] "Is not the history of Adam repeated in me?"'[4] Pseudo-Matthew adds other details: the maids who defend Mary's innocence and tell Joseph of the angel, his hilarious reply that 'some one hath feigned himself an angel of the Lord and deceived her,'[5] and, eventually, his humble apology to Mary: 'I have sinned, in that I had some suspicion of thee.'[6] Finally, while both of these sources add detail to the canonical accounts, the *Nativity of Mary* subtracts a key detail from the other apocrypha, as it alone 'refers to Joseph's great age but says nothing of his supposed previous marriage and other children.'[7] Thus the image of Joseph – the elderly, cranky newlywed, caught in a completely unexpected situation, with a great capacity for forgiveness when nudged – is between the three accounts mapped out for the medieval playwrights.

The question of Joseph's cult, and its influence upon the drama, is rather more complex. While it first began to develop in the twelfth century, it did not become widespread until the fifteenth; his feast day of 19 March entered the calendar in 1481, although it was not made a holy day of obligation until 1621.[8] Nonetheless many of his apologists and admirers were staunch indeed; in his second homily on the Annunciation, Bernard of Clairvaux declared,

> [E]x hac [...] meruit honorari a Deo, ut pater Dei et dictus, et creditus sit [...] non dubitas interpretari, qui et qualis homo fuerit iste Ioseph [...] tamquam alterum David Dominus invenit secundum cor tuum.

> From the fact that God allowed him to be called and thought of as father of the divine Child, you may judge how great a man Joseph was. [... In Joseph], as though he were another David, the Lord found a man after His own heart.[9]

In 1416, at the Council of Constance, Jean Gerson preached,

> Libet hic exclamare: o miranda prorsus, Joseph, sublimitas tua. O dignitas incomparabilis ut mater Dei, regina coeli, domina mundi, appelare te dominum non indignum putaverit. Nescio sane [...] quid hic amplius habeat mirabilis vel humilitas in Maria vel in Joseph sublimitas.

> Well may we exclaim at your wholly wonderful greatness, Joseph! What an unexampled distinction! – the Mother of God, the Queen of Heaven, the Mistress of the world, vouchsafed to call you her master. I do not know which excites the more wonder – Mary's humility or Joseph's exaltedness.[10]

Perhaps most revealing of all is the statement by Ubertino of Casale, later quoted by Bernardine of Siena, that Joseph

> est clausula Veteris Testamenti, in qua patriarchalis et prophetalis dignitas promissum consequitur fructum. Porro est hic solus, qui corporaliter possedit quod eis divina dignatio repromisit,

> is the key of the Old Testament, in whom the patriarchal and prophetical

dignity attained to its promised fruit. He alone, furthermore, possessed corporally what the Divine Majesty had promised to the fathers.[11]

Most such exaltation of Joseph during the late medieval period occurred on the Continent, and one cannot argue that these writings had a direct influence upon Joseph's portrayal in the Middle English drama. Nonetheless, there is evidence of a longstanding tradition of private if not public devotion to the saint in England, extending back to at least the twelfth century.[12] In addition, the ideas of such continental writers, especially Bernard, find analogues also in the *Meditationes vitae Christi*,[13] which in its English translation, Nicholas Love's *Mirror of the Blessed Life of Jesus Christ*, was among the most important English books of the period. Love refers to Joseph in a rather precise way, calling him 'wirschipful'[14] and also 'nyhe & acceptable to god,'[15] but noting also that he was not so exalted as the Virgin herself.[16] This is to say no more in an orthodox manner than that Joseph is a recognized saint, but the book's popularity and its inclusion of Joseph in the scenes for meditation may be seen as analogous to the portrayal of Joseph in the cycles, where, perhaps for the first time, the life of Joseph began to be a matter for public contemplation.

Joseph begins and is begun with principles that bear resemblance to those recommended by rhetoricians. In his *Poetria nova*, Geoffrey of Vinsauf argues that there are only a few ways in which to begin a story: one can begin with the beginning, with the middle, with the end, or with a proverb. Beginning at the beginning of the plot, Geoffrey tells us, is undesirable; the other combinations are classified as 'artistic,' and thus to be preferred.[17] The York Joseph, it is to be noted, is begun in the middle of the plot, rather than with the initial discovery of Mary's pregnancy. This fact makes him unique among his parallels. When the audience meets him, the York Joseph has gone through his initial shock, has questioned Mary, has decided to flee – and yet, in order for there to be a play at all, he must go back to speak to her again, as if to give her another chance. In addition, in order for the back-story to be known to the audience, Joseph must speak to them directly, and he does, so that the situation and his state of mind both become revealed at once.

Joseph begins by a simple yet complete portrayal of himself – both his current mood and his habitual nature. These two aspects of character were recognized in several writings on rhetoric, and indeed they formed a category of school exercise for centuries after their introduction into Latin thought by Priscian.[18] In addition to these two aspects of himself, Joseph also covers his manner of life, his fortunes, his habits, his feelings, interests, purposes, accidents, all in a manner that Cicero would have recognized. Yet whatever the influence or lack thereof of such writers upon the York playwright, there is no doubt that Joseph's initial speech is a seemingly oxymoronic marvel of encyclopaedic economy. More significant, however, is the way in which this play depicts Joseph as someone torn between legalistic and domestic interests, and that it does so by contextualizing the domestic within the legalistic. So far, these contentions may seem obvious. What is perhaps less obvious is the series of roles in which the audience itself is placed in reaction to these roles of Joseph. First as potentially hostile jurors, then as spying onlookers, finally as fellow Christians with Joseph, the audience gradually grows nearer to the character over the course of the play, or perhaps one should say finds the character growing closer to them, as the spheres of legality and domesticity become reconciled and, ultimately, sanctified. While most literary characters on their first appearance have no immediate history, that is not true of biblical characters in relation to the audience, whose horizon of expectations has been established already. Nonetheless, even biblical characters are malleable, and the way in which the appeal to the expectations of the audience can vary widely.

For example, Joseph may well make his initial appearance before the wagon rolls into place,[19] thus appearing alone before a crowd of onlookers, as the doctor in the previous Annunciation play may have done. Joseph's rhetoric instantly demands the listeners' attention, and demands also active participation in the resolution of the judicial questions of his and Mary's innocence or guilt. Joseph begins the play like a hunted man and like a conscious rhetor also, excusing his appearance before the audience with a *purgatio in necessitate*,[20] explaining that his age prevents any more dignified appearance:

> For nowe þan wende I best hafe bene
> > Att ease and reste by reasoune ay.
> > > For I am of grete elde,
> > > Wayke and al vnwelde,
> > > As ilke man se it maye;
> > > > I may nowder buske ne belde
> > > > But owther in frithe or felde;
> > > For shame what sall I saie[?]   (York 13/3–10)

Unlike the doctor who has dazzled the audience with his willing rhetoric in the preceding 'Annunciation' play, Joseph seems to have been dragged on unwillingly to face a jury of his peers, and peers who have already been convinced of his guilt. 'Si persuasus auditor, si oratio adversariorum fecerit fidem auditoribus [...] dubitatione utemur quid potissimum dicamus aut cui loco primum respondeamus, cum admiratione.' (If the hearers have been convinced, if our opponent's speech has gained their credence [...] we shall use Indecision, along with an exclamation of astonishment: 'What had I best say?' or 'To what point shall I first reply?').[21] By positing the need for an excuse, and for the need to gain the audience's sympathy rather than being presumed to have it, Joseph not only casts himself in the role of accused, but also casts the audience in the role of hostile jury. In addition, the use of questions, even rhetorical ones, explicitly invites the audience to make judgments. Such a tactic is similar to that at the end of the Brome 'Abraham and Isaac' play, when the doctor asks the audience,

> Trowe 3e, sorys, and God sent an angell
> And commawndyd 3ow 3owre chyld to slayn,
> Be 3owre trowthe ys ther ony of 3ow
> That eyther wold groche or stryve therageyn?
> How thyngke 3e now, sorys, therby?
> I trow ther be thre ore a fowr or moo.   (443–8)[22]

It is of course an open question whether the audience is willing to play that role. But Joseph's rhetoric, with its questioning and its musing about what other people will do to him, forces a fictional audience to arise; the audience becomes aware that Joseph is talking about them. The audience thus begins to have a split role – partly faithful Christians beholding their sacred history, and partly people sitting in judgment.

Thus Joseph instantly creates a kind of ritual space *for* the process of judgment. Within that space, the fictional audience is hoped to be attentive and sympathetic to Joseph's case. Accordingly, Joseph follows this opening or *insinuatio* with *narratio*, or recounting of the facts. During his monologue, he constantly stresses his lack of guilt by claiming necessity or lack of understanding: 'I ne wist what it ment' (York 13/30), '[T]hay saide to me forthy/Þat with a wiffe I sulde be wedde' (York 13/33–4), 'I am begiled – how, wate I no3t' (York 13/42), 'To gabbe yf I wolde payne me,/Þe lawe standis harde agayne me' (York

13/48–9). Thus Joseph excuses himself for marrying someone much younger than himself, for her unexpected pregnancy, and for his appearance before this jury in full admission of the facts. The audience becomes aware of a role that they perhaps do not wish to play. They begin to perceive Joseph's spiritual blindness as a form of misinterpretation of themselves. Their role as faithful Christians is challenged by the role of judges that Joseph's rhetoric foists upon them.

Yet sprinkled throughout this extended *purgatio* are references to other actions for which Joseph does take responsibility, and for which he asks no judgment: 'And lathe methinkeþ, on þe todir syde,/My wiff with any man to defame' (York 13/51–2); 'Of my wendyng wil I non warne,/Neuere þe lees it is myne entente/To aske hir who gate hir þat barne,/Ʒitt wolde I witte fayne or I wente' (York 13/71–4). These statements refer specifically to Mary's character and actions, rather than to the brute facts of her biological state. They thus begin to cast Joseph in a different light from before: now he is playing the role of guardian, even if it is a guardian who is thinking of fleeing his charge.

Thus Joseph begins also to entertain thoughts relating not to the juridical sphere but to the domestic; and in that sphere the audience has a very different set of roles. Joseph's statements that he will tell nobody about either Mary's pregnancy or his flight belie, for the first time, the audience's presence. Thus the audience is no longer in the role, exactly, of jurors; or, rather, that role has had an additional nuance added to it. Now they are disembodied spectators, overhearing the play rather than immediately participating in it. They are, perhaps, engaging in a particularly concretized form of visualization such as that recommended by such devotional works as the *Meditationes vitae Christi*. If so, then their role as faithful Christians is now buttressed rather than subverted, and yet they do not yet lose their role as judges, because the issues that Joseph has raised have not yet been resolved by the play's plot.

While this monologue has been going on, the wagon has most probably rolled up and been set up. Thus the ritual juridical space created by Joseph's oration has been disrupted by the introduction of domestic space. Now, when Joseph goes into his house, the audience will go with him, as spectators overhearing and yet still judging the events before them.

Joseph, upon entering the house, begins with a line that will become typical of the character from that point through the rest of the cycle: 'All hayle, God be herinne' (13/75). It seems a straightforward enough greeting, yet it also says far more than the character would seem to intend. The first two words, 'All hayle,' echo the angel's greeting of Mary, while the three remaining words, 'God be herinne,' state the miraculous fact that will exonerate both Joseph and Mary and indeed the rest of humanity: God is indeed herein, both within Mary and within the house, and, by extension, within the place where the play is enacted. This *significatio per ambiguum*[23] is used for the conveyance of divine truths of which Joseph is not aware. The same happens with Joseph's question to the maids, 'Whare is þat ȝonge virgine/Marie, my berde so bright?' (York 13/77–8). What seems to be an intended *antiphrasis* is, in fact, a literal description of one of Mary's most important characteristics, her perpetual virginity. The character is thus placed in the light of a particular form of dramatic irony, one in which he remains for the rest of his portrayal in the York Cycle. Joseph seems to be guided by Providence without knowing it.

This dramatic irony is triggered in Joseph by his actual attempts to interact with Mary; those attempts continue to trigger responses in Joseph that undermine his ability to accuse his wife. Although he asks her the direct question, 'Whose ist Marie?' (York 13/103) in some form or other six times, and receives some variation on 'Sir, Goddis and youres' (York 13/103) an equal number of times, he is not able to direct much more than that against her. His opening gambit to Mary, far from being neat or focused, is instead a mess of indirection:

Gramercy Marie, saie what chere,
  Telle me soth, how est with þe?
    Wha has ben there?
  Thy wombe is waxen grete, thynke me,
    Þou arte with barne, allas for care.
      A, maidens, wa worthe ȝou,
      Þat lete hir lere swilke lare.   (York 13/92–8)

A mixture of pleasantries, direct but awkward questioning, a statement of very obvious fact followed by a completely unnecessary qualification by opinion, another statement of very obvious fact followed by an exclamation of woe, and finally a *categoria* directed not at Mary but at her maids – all of it adds up not to an effective accusation, but instead to an expression of *pathos* bordering on *bathos*.

In modern performance, such as one directed by myself in Toronto in 1995, the *pathos* does indeed seem to topple over into *bathos*. The modern audience laughs at Joseph's consternation rather than weeping at it, and no wonder. Whether the medieval audience did so is another matter. Arnold Williams has noted how difficult it is to be sure: 'Comedy is notoriously subject to the accidents of time and space. [...] It is quite possible that what we see as funny was utterly serious' to the medieval audience, as nineteenth-century melodrama seems to have been taken seriously by its audiences but is considered camp today.[24] Nonetheless, the scenes of Joseph's consternation may well have been funny to a medieval audience for the following reason alone: there is in fact nothing for Joseph to weep about, though he does not know it. Mary is, of course, telling the truth, and Joseph is, indeed, 'begiled,' though not in the way in which he thinks. Jauss observes: 'The comic hero is not comic in himself but against the horizon of certain expectations; he is comic because he negates those expectations or norms.'[25] By making Joseph funny, the playwright calls attention to those expectations and norms and reinforces them through laughter at the one who negates – or tries to negate – them.

It would be easy to dismiss Joseph as a mere fool at this point, but to do so would ignore the skilful way in which the text, which has worked to alienate the audience, also works to draw them in.

[*Joseph.*]	But who is þe fader? Telle me his name.
Maria.	None but yourselfe.
Joseph.	Late be, for shame.
	I did it neuere; þou dotist dame, by bukes and belles!
	Full sakles shulde I bere þis blame aftir þou telles
	. . . .
	Yhitt for myn awne I wolde it fede,
	Might all be still;
	Þarfore þe fadir tell me, Marie.
Maria.	But God and yhow, I knaw right nane.
Joseph.	A, slike sawes mase me full sarye,
	With grete mornyng to make my mane. (York 13/177–80, 185–90)

Joseph's lines run on hypermetrically for the first and only time in the play, an indication of a loss of temper and control.[26] Yet Joseph also attempts to make peace, offering to care for the child 'for myn awne.' Later, he also assures Mary, 'Sertis, þer sall none witte but we./I drede þe law als wele as thou' (York 13/199–200). In these lines, Joseph attempts to identify himself, in the Burkean sense,[27] with Mary, by asserting that his interests are the same as hers: care of the child, and fear of the law. His failure lies in the fact that Mary has no fear of the law because of her child. In failing to identify Mary as the 'maiden to be with childe' (York 13/211) of prophecy – 'Sho is not borne I wene,' he says (York 13/213) – Joseph casts himself in the wrong role, as cuckold, and leaves himself no ability to overcome his alienation from Mary through conscious identification. He cannot understand her situation and therefore her motives.

The audience, of course, knows of Mary's situation but, through Joseph's confusion, is made sharply aware that they cannot understand it either, at least not through logic. Only through faith is comprehension of the Incarnation possible; the failure of Joseph to understand, based upon his legalistic and domestic premises, demonstrates the fact vividly, as does the subsequent visit by the angel, which miraculously clarifies matters.

When this visitation happens, Joseph's reconciliation with Mary also occurs. Rosemary Woolf declares that this little scene 'is too perfunctorily done to deserve mention,'[28] but in performance it can be deeply moving because of, not despite, its brevity. Joseph, in planning his apology, notes, 'Me bus pray hir halde me excused,/Als som men dose with full gud chere' (York 13/288–9); thus he once again acknowledges the audience's presence, though obliquely. Also, since the angel's appearance to Joseph, the audience's original horizon of expectations regarding the virginity of Mary has been reaffirmed, and Joseph has shared in that reaffirmation. Thus the audience does not identify with Joseph per se; rather, Joseph has been identified with the audience. The audience's roles as jurors and overseers have been exploded, and now Joseph, having moved from accused to guardian to member of the faithful, is ready to play a new set of roles that combine all of the spheres of which his character has had a part: 'Marie, I am to blame,' juridical, 'gadir same now all oure gere,' domestic, 'Till Bedlem bus me it bere,' sacramental. Joseph is not only 'there to turn the theological mystery of the Incarnation into a homely, human event,'[29] but also to turn homely, human events into the contexts for that theological mystery, and to show their limitations at the same time. The audience's roles in the juridical and domestic spheres, like Joseph's roles, give way before their role as faithful Christians.

In identifying Joseph with the audience, the play brings his expectations into line with theirs; through the temporary splitting and reconciliation of theirs, it also brings relief and reassures them that their original set of beliefs and expectations regarding the Virgin Birth and the Incarnation of God are indeed valid; yet it also shows that those expectations and beliefs are a matter of faith and not reason. Thus, the play of 'Joseph's Trouble about Mary' is a subtle and masterful piece of theatrical and devotional rhetoric, reassuring where people may not even have thought that they needed reassurance, and thus positing that they did whether or not they had thought so. Ultimately, the audience plays the role of faithful Christians in need of reassurance, and Joseph plays the role of one whose conversion provides that reassurance.

This role continues and expands throughout the rest of Joseph's story within the York Cycle. In 'The Nativity' and in the late 'Purification,' Joseph helps to provide interpretive links between the action on stage and analogous rites and rituals known to the audience; his reactions serve as gloss to both. A key difference between the earlier play and the later, however, is the apparent lack of awareness Joseph displays in the latter of the audience's presence. Much of his role in this respect is taken over by Simeon, Anna, and the Priest, a reflection, perhaps, of the changing public perception of, and increasing devotion to, the saint.[30]

Joseph's next appearance in the cycle, at the beginning of 'The Nativity,' continues to create a tension between the world of the play and the world of the audience, and to induce implied roles for the audience to play, roles that emphasize the need for faith and place faith firmly within earthly contexts.

Joseph's opening lines in the play posit the audience as present but unaware of the characters' true situation; referring to 'þis place where we are pight,/Oureself allone' (York 14/4–5), he nonetheless declares that 'So mekill pepull is comen to towne/Þat we can nowhere herbered be,/Þer is slike prees' (York 14/10–12). The audience here is cast in the role of an ignorant crowd milling about an ordinary-looking couple, neither aware of nor concerned about the pregnant woman with no place to harbour herself. Because the real audience knows the story, this is most likely not a role that they might have been willing to play; nonetheless, it is the role that is implied.

The audience's separation from the characters extends to the moment of the Nativity itself. The staging of this moment is not entirely clear from the manuscript; the only indications are Mary's dialogue. Without any particular warning, she exclaims:

Jesu my son þat is so dere,
Nowe borne is he.

Hayle my lord God, hayle prince of pees,
  Hayle my fadir, and hayle my sone;
Hayle souereyne sege all synnes to sesse.   (York 14/55–9)

Mary continues with a series of such panegyric lines. The Christ child's
first appearance is certainly on the ground, for Mary shortly afterwards asks, 'Vowchesaffe, swete sone I pray þe,/That I myght þe take
in þe armys of myne' (York 14/65–6). This lifting of the Christ child
may have had mnemonic resonances with the Mass; if it is so that 'all
late medieval bodily feasts of Mary [are] also meditation on the gift,
both joyful and sorrowful, of *corpus Christi*,'[31] then Mary's elevation of
the Christ child into visibility may have had an effect reminiscent of
that of the elevation of the Host.

The sacramental moment echoed here is a moment of tension as well
as holiness. The visible evidence of the Host was paramount to the
faith of the medieval Christian – indeed, it was the moment of communion for most lay people most of the time – but it was also the occasion of doubts because, after all, '[t]he Host did not look like the thing
it was': a problem that occupied much of late medieval Eucharistic
thought.[32] Joseph's role in the Nativity play, like his role in the
'Joseph's Trouble' play, is to negotiate that confusion, and to enable the
audience to place itself in a position of faith.

Mary's delivery of Christ takes place before the eyes of the audience
but out of the sight of Joseph, whose concern at the moment of Christ's
birth is not exactly worldly, but certainly material:

A, lorde God what þe wedir is colde,
  Þe fellest freese þat euere I felyd.
I pray God helpe þam þat is alde
  And namely þam þat is vnwelde,
    So may I saie.
  Now gud God þou be my bilde
    As þou best may.   (York 14/71–7)

Here, Joseph's concern is related to the protective, domestic sphere that
was so important to the character in his initial appearance. It also provides an additional fictionalizing element and makes further demands
upon the audience's imagination of themselves. The actual performance of the play, of course, took place in late May or in June. By
remarking on the coldness of the weather, Joseph invites the audience

to imagine themselves not only as the unseeing crowd of the play's introduction, but also as fellow sufferers at the hands of the elements. For a medieval populace in a northern region, whose experiences of winter were without the amenities of modern technology, such an imaginative projection must not have been too great a strain. Joseph's invocation of the physical at the moment of Christ's birth is not, however, a mere aspect of the appearance of 'natural man,'[33] still less a symbol of spiritual blindness. Rather, as a rhetorical strategy it emphasizes the physicality of the event and therefore of Christ's humanity, like the more famous complaints about winter's cold in the Towneley 'Second Shepherd's Play.'[34] Joseph, then, invites the audience to put aside the present experience of their own senses, and to participate imaginatively in the experience of Christ's incarnation.

Appropriately, Joseph's complaint about the cold is juxtaposed with his sudden observation of the light of salvation:

> A, lord God, what light is þis
>   Þat comes shynyng þus sodenly?
> I can not saie als haue I blisse.
>   When I come home vnto Marie
>   Þan sall I spirre.   (York 14/78–82)

Joseph is at this time in a different relationship to the audience than at the beginning of the play. Then, he posited the audience as unseeing while he remained aware of the situation; now, those roles are reversed. By wondering at the light, by declaring that he does not know or understand, Joseph reinforces the point that the audience has, on the other hand, seen; thus he serves to shore up the implied audience's position of faith by contrast with himself.

That contrast is not based, however, upon a lack of faith on Joseph's part; rather, it is based upon his simple lack of knowledge through experience. Upon Joseph's return, he appears not to notice what has happened at first; upon discovering the truth, his reaction is not one of disbelief but rather of surprise.

> *Joseph.*   Say Marie, doghtir, what chere with þe?
> *Maria.*   Right goode Joseph, as has been ay.
> *Joseph.*   O Marie, what swete thyng is þat on thy kne?
> *Maria.*   It is my sone, þe soth to saye,
>   Þat is so gud.

Joseph.　　　Wele is me I bade þis day
　　　　　　　To se þis foode.　　　　　　　　　　　　(York 14/85–91)

Joseph now comes belatedly into the position into which he and Mary have already induced the audience: into that of a witness to Christ's nativity.

As in 'Joseph's Trouble,' it is not the case that the audience identifies with Joseph per se; rather, Joseph and Mary manoeuvre the implied audience into a position with which Joseph is subsequently identified. The identification of Joseph with the audience is then exploited in a formal expression of faith, one of many such *laudationes* of Christ in the York Cycle:

Nowe welcome, floure fairest of hewe,
　I shall þe menske with mayne and myght.
Hayle my maker, hayle Crist Jesu,
　Hayl riall kyng, roote of all right,
　　Hayle saueour,
　Hayle my lorde, lemer of light,
　　Hayle blessid floure.　　　　　　　　　　　　(York 14/106–12)

Like its analogues in the cycle, Joseph's *laudatio* uses alliteration of soft consonants, *anaphora, expolitio, exclamatio* – in short, numerous rhetorical devices in a very compressed space – to achieve a mixture of formal elegance and a high emotional pitch. In particular, the repetitive devices are a kind of verbal analogue to the idea of divine stillness which underlies all medieval drama.[35] That stillness is underpinned by the next appearance of Joseph, and of Mary, during 'The Shepherds,' in which the silence of the Holy Family eerily foreshadows the silence of Christ during the York Cycle's long trial sequence.

During the brief remainder of 'The Nativity,' Joseph observes the behaviour of the ox and the ass (York 14/122–6), interprets a prophecy of Habbakuk regarding those beasts (York 14/137–41), and, subsequently, dedicates himself to the Christ child. In other words, Joseph acts as one who weighs evidence and comes to a personal decision. In doing so, he seems to take the opposite course from Augustine's advice, '[N]oli quaerere intelligere, ut credas, sed crede ut intelligas' (Do not seek to understand in order to believe; but believe in order to understand).[36] Yet Joseph's declaration is not one of initial faith; Joseph's faith preceded the event of Christ's nativity, as we have already seen. Rather, it is a declaration of loyalty to his lord, and an invitation to the audience to make similar declarations themselves. Furthermore, Joseph's process of arriving at that declaration – that of faith based on signs and authorities – is one that Augustine himself understood very well.[37]

> Honnoure and worshippe both day and nyght,
>> Ay-lastand lorde, be done to þe
>>> Allway, as is worthy;
>> And lord, to thy seruice I oblissh me
>>> With all myn herte, holy. (York 14/143–7)

Joseph plays a peculiar role in the Holy Family, at least as portrayed in the York Cycle. If Christ is the Saviour Incarnate and Mary the Divine Virgin, then Joseph is the first Christian. Lacking the direct bodily experiences of the divine of both of the other two, absent from both the beginning and end of Mary's pregnancy, Joseph has no choice but to follow faith based on signs and authorities.

'The Flight into Egypt,' in contrast, finds Joseph dwelling on his own helplessness. As in his ruminations at the beginning of 'Joseph's Trouble,' Joseph's opening speech notes his 'sympplenes' and claims, 'I waxe as wayke as any wande,/For febill me fayles both foote and hande' (York 18/16, 17–18). But he also notes his reliance on God more strongly than in previous appearances, and in a way that is different from what the audience has seen of him before.

> Thow maker þat is most of myght,
>> To thy mercy I make my mone;
> Lord, se vnto þis symple wight
>> Þat hase non helpe but þe allone.
>>> For all þis worlde I haue forsaken,
>>> And to thy seruice I haue me taken
>>> With witte and will
>>> For to fulfill
>>>> Þi commaundement. (York 18/1–9)

This opening speech is similar in several respects to those of Noah, Abraham, and Moses in the York Cycle's Old Testament plays: beginning with an alliterating epithet to God, it continues with a claim of dependence upon him, and notes the difficulties that the speaker faces.

Unlike those speeches, however, it does not contain a statement of the character's history, or of thanks for God's help. In the former case, such a statement is needless given the audience's long acquaintance with Joseph; in the second, it is this episode that will supply the occasion for such a statement. In this episode, the audience witnesses Joseph, whom it now knows as humble, multifaceted, an expert in the Law and a bridge to the Gospels, as he becomes the equivalent of an Old Testament patriarch.

While Joseph prays to God the Father, Mary prays to her son, God Incarnate. Such a difference may seem to signal a kind of gap between the old and new dispensations, but any such distinction soon becomes blurred. For the first time, Joseph becomes the centre of the action, when the angel appears not to Mary but to him (York 18/37–62). Following the warning to flee from Egypt, Joseph speaks two stanzas that reinforce his previously created position as a legalistic thinker and a domestic actor:

> Aye-lastand lord, loved mott þou be
>> That thy swete sande wolde to me sende.
> But lorde, what ayles þe kyng at me,
>> For vnto hym I neuere offende?
>
> . . . .
>> As worthy is
>> Þou kyng of blisse,
>>> Þi will be wrought.
>>> Marie my doughtir dere,
>> On þe is all my þought.   (York 18/63–6, 81–5)

While it may seem at first that Joseph's question, '[W]hat ayles þe kyng at me[?]' is a minor example of blindness – it is, after all, the child and not the stepfather that the king wishes to kill – it is really not so. Instead, Joseph's dwelling on his specific innocence in relation to the king, and on the a priori innocence of 'Smale 3onge barnes þat neuere did ille,' shows a concern with different forms of culpability; his turning to Mary, his 'doughtir,' again recalls his role, both legal and domestic, that the audience already knows. But the key feature of Joseph's speech is pathetic. By lamenting his fate, by portraying the innocence of children, by turning to the Virgin with the words, 'Þe chere of me is done for ay' (York 18/87), Joseph invites the audience to step into the scene and lament with him. Joseph does not directly manipulate the audience by referring them into different roles; on the contrary, in none of the speeches in the play does Joseph even acknowledge the audience's presence. While the York Cycle's strong sense of place does, perhaps, place the audience implicitly in the role of other endangered families, this is not the primary form of manipulation. Rather, the manipulation comes from the invitation to sympathy that runs throughout the play. While Joseph's anguish in 'Troubles' is ironic, and while Mary has until now remained self-contained and aloof from trouble, the events of this play bring them both for the first time into real danger and emotional anguish, an opportunity of which the playwright makes the greatest effect.

Joseph once again employs means to move the audience that ancient rhetoricians would have recognized; the *Rhetorica ad Herennium* states baldly enough, 'Conquestio est oratio quae incommodorum amplificatione animum auditoris ad misericordiam perducit' (The Pathetic, by amplifying misfortunes, wins the hearer over to pity).[38] Joseph indeed multiplies misfortunes and also tidings of misfortunes in this play. He repeats or alludes to, no less than six times, the news that Herod is about to slaughter children (York 18/67–70, 101–2, 111–12, 115–20, 150–5, 160–1); he mentions his sadness at being exiled and his fear of lingering (York 18/90–3, 132–4); he reminds the audience of his willingness to bear all burdens despite his weakness (York 18/164–70); he admits, most pathetically of all, that he has no idea where Egypt is (York 18/179–80). Cumulatively, he builds up a self-portrait of seeming helplessness.

Of course, Joseph is not the only one to do so. The helplessness in Mary's portrait is even stronger, and is in direct contrast to the confident, even aloof, character that the Virgin has heretofore seemed in the York Cycle. No longer the seemingly unmoveable and inscrutable being of 'Joseph's Trouble,' she is overcome with emotion, becoming an image for the first time of the sorrowful Virgin of the Crucifixion. Her fear paralyses her, however, preventing her from taking any useful action; all she is able to do is to 'durk, [...] dare' (York 18/106), and lament:

[*Maria*.]	I ware full wille of wane
	My sone and he shulde dye,
	And I haue but hym allone.
Joseph.	We, leue Marie, do way, late be!
	I pray þe, leue of thy dynne,
	And fande þe furthe faste for to flee. (York 18/144–9)

Joseph's response to Mary's helplessness is to take charge himself of the situation; his doing so climaxes in an astonishing iconographic moment.

[*Joseph.*]	Gyff me hym, late me bere hym awhile.
Maria.	I thanke you of youre grete goode dede;
	Now gud Joseph tille hym take hede
	· ·
Joseph.	Late me and hym allone. (York 18/198–200, 204)

The effect of Joseph's taking the Christ child in his arms is somewhat difficult to describe. Near the beginning of the play, John Clerke wrote, 'This matter is mayd of newe after anoþer form'; this note was later crossed out.[39] If Clerke was initially citing accurate information, then the play as we have it is a mid-sixteenth-century revision. Such a date might make sense, given that portrayals of Joseph with the Christ child in his arms seem first to have emerged around that time.[40] Of course, the detail may also be a response to a practical problem. Since the play specifies that the actor playing Mary must ride off (presumably on a donkey), holding on 'faste by þe mane' (York 18/206), the traditional picture of the Virgin riding while holding the child may have been found impossible to stage. Nonetheless, the image of Joseph holding the child while leading the donkey and Virgin remains; Mary has been reduced even further to a pathetically helpless figure than Joseph, while Joseph takes the lead, strengthened not by himself but by God: 'I haue oure helpe here in myn arme' (York 18/224).

That the first real danger that Christ faces should be the subject of *pathos*, and thus an occasion for affectivity, is hardly surprising. But it is not yet Christ who is the actor in the drama of *pathos*; Joseph and Mary, rather, must fulfil that place in their respective ways. In their helplessness, they invite the kind of pity that Nicholas Love recommends: 'Lord how dide þei þere of hire lyuelode, or where rested þei & were herbored in þe ny3tes, for in þat wey fonde þei ful seldome any house. Here ought we to haue inwardly compassion of hem, & no3t be loþe or þenk trauailous to do penance for our self siþen oþer token so gret & so oft trauaile for vs, namely þei þat weren so noble & so worþi.'[41] Furthermore, they do so, as we have seen, through the multiplying of woes that ancient rhetoricians recommended, and through a final, almost belated reference to the audience's presence.

[*Joseph.*]   Late vs goo with good chere –
          Farewele and haue gud day –
          God blisse vs all in fere.
Maria. Amen as he beste may.   (York 18/228–31)

Referring to the audience not as 'you' but as 'us,' identifying the audience with themselves, Joseph and Mary beat a hasty retreat down the
streets of York, leaving some of the audience behind and, possibly, taking some with them. Yet in doing so, they create an implied community of pity around them. The audience, reminded however willingly
or reluctantly that the play is about 'us,' watches the pathetic refugees
go and prepares itself for the horrors that are to follow, both in the
Slaughter of the Innocents and, by implication, in the later Passion
sequence. If the audience may have been less reluctant to play such a
role than certain others it has played, the violence of the following
'Slaughter' may make up for such willingness. Yet the audience also
will find that its identification with the Holy Family, and especially
with Joseph, is soon to be disengaged.
    The last York play in which Joseph appears, 'Christ and the Doctors,'
begins with a disorienting break in the action and chronology. The
audience has just witnessed the slaughter from which the Holy Family
has run away, a slaughter which the Holy Family has nonetheless
haunted verbally:

[*Maria.*] I ware full wille of wane
My sone and he shulde dye,
    And I have but hym allone.   (York 18/144–6)

[*Ii Mulier.*] Þe knyght vppon his knyffe
    Hath slayne my sone so swette,
        And I hadde but hym allone.   (York 19/213–15)

After this slaughter and the laments of the mothers, Joseph and Mary
reappear, casually walking down the streets without their son, speaking at their ease:

Joseph. Marie, of mirthis we may vs mene,
    And trewly telle betwixte vs twoo
Of solempne sightis þat we haue sene
    In þat cité where we come froo.

Maria. Sertis Joseph, ȝe will noȝt wene
　What myrthis within my harte I maie,
Sen þat oure sone with vs has bene
　And sene ther solempne sightis alswae.　　　　　　　　　　　(York 20/1–8)

The break signals the end of one sequence in the York Cycle and the beginning of another; it also permits, indeed induces, the audience to readjust its thinking about the play, becoming newly aware of its dramaturgy and structure. Through his brief appearances in this play, Joseph guides the audience through this readjustment.

He does so by speaking in ways that point to different aspects of the dramatic situation simultaneously. Upon her discovery that Jesus is missing, Mary immediately repeats the same panicky behaviour as in 'The Flight into Egypt': 'A, sir, where is oure semely sone?/I trowe oure wittis be waste and wynde./Allas, in bale þus am I boone' (York 20/15–17). Joseph replies, not by partaking of her grief, but by making an observation that is at once scriptural, dramaturgical, and literary:

Marie, mende thy chere,
　For certis what all is done
He comes with folke in feere,
　And will ouertake vs sone.　　　　　　　　　　　　　　　　　(York 20/21–4)

Scripturally, this observation echoes the detail that Joseph and Mary at first thought *'illum esse in comitatu,'* 'that he was in the company' just behind them (Luke 2:44). Dramaturgically, it is a statement of a literal fact: the actor(s) playing Jesus, and the various 'folke in feere' of the subsequent plays, are indeed just behind the actors playing Joseph and Mary, and will indeed overtake them in less than fifty lines – perhaps three minutes of playing time. Indeed, the audience would almost certainly, at certain stations, have been able to see or hear the 'feere' approaching at that moment. Finally, it is also true that this play marks the end of the infancy narrative and the beginning of Christ's ministry, so that Jesus alone will soon 'ouertake' and surpass the Holy Family in both literary and theological senses.

This heavily polyvalent quatrain is not only a reply to Mary's panic but also a reply to the audience's possible reactions. Reminding them of the dramaturgical reality of the play, and also of the importance of Christ, Joseph prepares the audience to disengage its full attention from the story of the Holy Family, so that it can focus instead upon the story of Christ's ministry and passion. This process continues through the first section of the play; while Mary continues to cry out pathetic appeals, Joseph provides suggestions of action, all of which emphasize the need to search for Christ, and the surety of finding him:

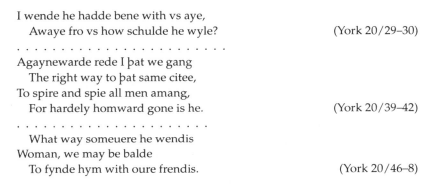

> I wende he hadde bene with vs aye,
> > Awaye fro vs how schulde he wyle?   (York 20/29–30)
>
> . . . .
>
> Agaynewarde rede I þat we gang
> > The right way to þat same citee,
> To spire and spie all men amang,
> > For hardely homward gone is he.   (York 20/39–42)
>
> . . . .
>
> > What way someuere he wendis
> Woman, we may be balde
> > To fynde hym with oure frendis.   (York 20/46–8)

Joseph's reassurances to Mary, of course, are directly based on Scripture; they are also, however, answers to the emotional response not only of Mary but also of the audience. After the emotional appeals of the 'Slaughter,' the audience may be prepared to react in the same way to the emotional appeals of Mary in this play, and to re-enact the emotional prefiguring of Christ's eventual sacrifice. But literally, there *is* no danger; Christ is merely speaking with the doctors in the temple. Consequently, while Joseph's assurances have the same note of authority as his taking command in the 'Flight into Egypt,' they have none of the same emotional appeal. The disparity between the emotion portrayed on the stage, and that encouraged to develop in the audience, leads the audience to accept that the role of the Holy Family is coming to a close; affectivity with the Holy Family no longer provides a sure guide to the events to come.

Following the scene in the temple, in which Christ appears for the first time as a speaking being, Joseph returns with Mary for his last appearance in the York Cycle. In his final scene, he completes his disengagement, and takes his leave. He accomplishes the former by reminding the audience of his temporal, human side, protesting that he cannot speak with the doctors in the temple because 'They are so gay in furres fyne' and because 'I can nowthir croke nor knele' (York 20/232, 240). His poverty and age are reasserted for the first time in a long while, as is his concern with law. His awareness of the earthly laws of propriety, and his fleshly feebleness, will not allow him to make the final journey to find Christ again without the help of Mary. Again, Joseph becomes manipulated into a position in which he is identified with humanity in general, and therefore with the audience.

Joseph's final farewell to the audience allows him to close the story of the Holy Family, and also to hand over the rest of the Cycle to Christ: 'No lenger will we bide,/Fares wele all folke in feere' (York 20/ 287–8). From here on, the cycle will focus on Jesus' own actions, and the audience, prepared by the story of the Holy Family, must use what it has thus far assimilated to experience the central story of the cycle.

Joseph's journey as the first Christian takes on a different form in 'The Purification.' This play, as it now exists in the York Register, is a very late version, entered after 1567, although a version of the play is recorded as having existed as early as 1415.[42] Since this play is so much later than that, we must keep in mind that the characterization of Joseph in the episode may have changed significantly over the intervening century and a half. But the most significant change that certainly took place over that period was the Reformation, and the resulting implications regarding the importance, forms, and meaning of the ritual of the purification of women must be taken into account.

The politics of such a play in 1567 are ambiguous. The ritual for purification or churching outlined in the *Book of Common Prayer* has not changed much since its inception, but during the sixteenth century the emphasis on purification was lessened, while that of thanksgiving was increased. For example, the prayer book of 1549 entitles the ritual 'The Order of the Purification of Weomen' while the revised book of 1552 changes the title to 'The Thankes Geuing of Women after Childe Birth, Commonly Called the Churchyng of Women.'[43] In addition, the more radical Protestants of the time objected to any emphasis on purification at all (and often to any churching ritual of any kind) as being not only too Catholic but too Jewish, calling it among other things 'a mixed action of Judaism and popery.'[44] Their argument was not popular; most women seem to have used the Common Prayer ritual without any negative feelings about its Judaic origins.[45] In fact, Keith Thomas argues that 'for people at large churching was indubitably [...] closely linked to its Jewish predecessor,' and that that link with the sacred past was considered positive – though not all scholars share Thomas's view.[46]

Thus, the habitual entitling of the play as 'the Purificacion of our lady,'[47] Mary and Joseph's debate over the need for, and meaning of, the ritual, and Joseph's rhetorical and exegetical linking of the Jewish laws to Christian fulfilment can perhaps be seen as a late example of the York plays' assertion and reinforcement of a lasting community. For all the religious changes that had taken place in the preceding decades, the ritual of churching remained central to community life; it was the moment in which a woman, recently separated from the community by her childbearing, was brought back in. It was also a moment of reinforcement of ecclesiastical authority over the life of the community, and, from a certain point of view, of the link between Christian life and its ancient past.[48]

Joseph's role in the portrayal of this moment differs somewhat from his role in earlier York plays. For example, 'The Purification' is unusual in that it does not necessarily, to a modern reader, portray Joseph as an old man. He is wise in the law, to be sure, as his ability to recite significant details of it from memory indicates, but he does not ever complain about his physical condition or refer to his age (such complaints in this play are reserved for Simeon). Furthermore, he refers to Mary as 'spowse' (York 17/200) rather than 'doghter,' his more usual appellation for her. In fact, Joseph usually did not become portrayed as a young man in art until the seventeenth century,[49] and the inclusion of this character in the York Cycle, amidst five other, traditional Josephs, makes it highly unlikely that this Joseph is a young man. The difference seems to result from a different understanding of Joseph's age: not feeble, but venerable.

The first words spoken of Joseph are Mary's address to him, 'Joseph my husbonde and my feer' (York 17/187). The description of him as 'feer' or companion is in some contrast to Mary's address of him in the earlier plays of the cycle; indeed, her customary appellation, 'Sir,' is not to be found in 'The Purification' at all. The difference not only signifies a somewhat more assertive characterization of Mary, but also a different relationship between her and Joseph; not her guardian but her companion and adviser, he represents a bridge between the old law and the new, between the characters on the stage, and between the audience and the scene.

Joseph is seen, first, to be an expert in the law of the temple. Indeed, he is far more expert in these matters than his spouse (rather a different situation from, say, that in the N-Town plays). When Mary first mentions that she wishes for purification, Joseph replies that, from a legal point of view, such action is needless.

> This matter that thowe moves to me
> Is for all these women bedene
>> That has conceyved with syn fleshly
>>> To bere a chylde.
>
> ·
> But Mary, byrde, thowe neyd not soo
> For this cause to bee puryfyed, loo,
>> In Goddes temple.
> For certys thowe art a clene vyrgyn.   (York 17/201–4, 209–12)

Joseph recognizes the legal principle of purification and affirms it, but asserts that the facts of this case are not covered by the law. 'Mulier, si suscepto semine pepererit masculum, immunda erit septem diebus. [...] Cumque expleti fuerint dies purificationis eius [...] nec potuerit offerre agnum, sumet duos turtures vel duos pullos columbae' (If a woman *having received seed* shall bear a man child, she shall be unclean seven days. [...] And when the days of her purification are expired [...] and she is not able to offer a lamb, she shall take two turtles, or two young pigeons [Lev. 12:2,6,8; my emphasis]). Joseph clearly knows the rite well, including the seemingly gratuitous detail that the law is only for a woman who has received seed.

His understanding of the law is not merely detailed, however. He connects the detail of the uniqueness of Mary's conception of Christ to her moral as well as physical purity: 'For certys thowe arte a clene vyrgyn/For any thoght thy harte within' (York 17/213–14). Such emphasis on thought, the heart, and intention echoes Christ's Sermon on the Mount, in which such lessons as 'Audistis quia dictum est antiquis: Non moechaberis. Ego autem dico vobis, quoniam omnis qui viderit mulierem ad concupiscendum eam, iam moechatus est eam in corde suo' (You have heard that it was said to them of old: Thou shalt not commit adultery. But I say to you, that whosoever shall look on a woman to lust after her, hath already committed adultery with her in his heart [Matt. 5:27–8]) are asserted as fulfilments of the old law in the new law. Thus, Joseph's expertise in the Mosaic law is not one of pedantic detail only; rather, it is portrayed as an understanding that bridges the gap, for medieval Christians, between the Old Testament and the New.

Of course, his assertion that purification is needless for Mary does not prevail. The Virgin argues that she wishes to offer 'a sample of mekeness' (York 17/221), and Joseph quickly and willingly agrees.

After a brief discussion over the technicalities of the sacrifice, in which Joseph's knowledge of the fine points of the law is further conveyed (York 17/232–53), Joseph leaps into a quite astonishing explanation of the law through typology and Christian theology:

> And yf we haue not both in feer,
>> The lame, the burd, as ryche men haue,
> Thynke that vs must present here
>> Oure babb Jesus, as we voutsaue
>>> Before Godes sight.
>>>> He is our lamb Mary, kare the not.   (17/254–9)

The explanation of Jesus as the lamb and the sacrifice places Joseph fully in the middle of the old and new dispensations; his bridging of the two allows the audience to interpret both the play and their familiar purification rites as a link between the Judaic and the Christian, and between the past and present of the community.

Joseph is not, however, portrayed as consciously understanding the full implications of Christianity; nor indeed is Mary. Following the Luke account, they cannot be;[50] but the inclusion of such a fact at the end of a play in which Joseph has played such a crucial hermeneutic function is telling. For, Joseph once again falls short of full understanding, and seems, as in his earlier portrayals, to occupy a space between adherence to law and understanding of the spirit: a space that must be filled by trust and wonder.

> *Joseph*. Mary, my spowse and madyn mylde,
>> In hart I marvell here greatly
> Howe these folke spekes of our chylde.
>> They say and tells of great maistry
>>> That he shall doo.
> *Maria*. Yea certes, Joseph, I marvell also,
>> But I shall bere it full styll in mynde.
> *Joseph*. God geve hyme grace here well to do,
>> For he is comme of gentyll kynde.   (York 17/428–36)

Joseph's wonder at the words of the prophets show, for the first time in this play, a hermeneutic impasse that the character cannot bridge. His response contrasts with the audience, who, knowing the story of Christ, knows well what the prophets mean. In his final lines, Joseph

once again makes a statement that is more significant than it at first
appears; though it seems literally to refer to Jesus' Davidic ancestry, it
rather obviously also refers to his divine nature. Joseph demonstrates
once again the tendency to say more than he thinks he is saying; the
dramatic irony typical of this character demonstrates, true to form, a
posture of acceptance in the face of mystery, inviting the audience to
do the same. He also invites the audience to do with his words what he
cannot do with those of the prophets: interpret them. Nonetheless, his
actions suggest that whether the interpretation of signs and words is
effective or not, acceptance and faith are still the proper attitudes and
must prevail.

From what we have seen, it is clear that no one absolutely coherent
picture of the character of Joseph is drawn. Nevertheless, the audience
(and the modern reader) cannot help noticing certain commonalities
throughout. Joseph is often a centre of *pathos*; he is portrayed as venerable, an expert in the law, a bridge to the new dispensation who does
not always understand the implications of his own statements or
actions. He is concerned with domestic and juridical matters, and frequently demonstrates the limitations of them both. He often becomes
manipulated into direct identification with the audience, though the
dramatic irony inherent in his character often creates tension of the
opposite kind. Above all, he is a character who demands engagement
and interpretation, and who both bridges the gap between the audience and its sacred past and allows the audience room to reflect upon
its relation to that past.

5

Paul and the Rhetoric of Sainthood

Unsurprisingly, Paul of Tarsus, the first major Christian rhetorician, has lurked behind many of the texts discussed in this book. It is he, after all, who provided Christianity with the gentile emphasis that allowed it to become the religion of medieval Europe in the first place. It is also his writing in the New Testament that provides the locus of Augustine's analysis in the first Christian rhetorical guidebook, *De doctrina Christiana*. Because of his epistles, Paul would have been more clearly known to medieval playwrights than any other New Testament figure, including, arguably, Jesus himself. But his personality, and the central moment of his life, are captured most vividly in the story of his conversion in Acts 9, the very story that the writer of the Digby *Conversion of Saint Paul* and his revisers chose to tell. In their translation of that story onto the stage,[1] the original playwright and his revisers created a complex study in miniature of many of the issues of rhetoric, piety, and community that have underlaid all the texts discussed so far.

The understanding of language, and of audience, underlying *The Conversion of Saint Paul* is complex. From the beginning, the host Poeta draws a sharp distinction between the apodictic proof of Scripture and the nonapodictic proof of the play's spectacle; he also asserts the need for the audience to engage critically with what it sees in order to make and overcome that distinction:

Honorable frendys, besechyng yow of lycens
    To procede owur processe, we may [shew] vnder your correccyon,
The conuersyon of Seynt Paule, as þe Byble gyf experyens.
    Whoo lyst to rede þe booke *Actum Appostolorum,*
    Ther shall he haue þe very notycyon;

But, as we can, we shall vs redres,
    Brefly, wyth yowur fauour, begynyng owur proces.   (7–13)

Poeta makes reference to this distinction throughout the play, declaring for instance that 'To vnderstande þis matter, wo lyst to rede /The Holy Bybyll for þe better spede,/ Ther shall he haue þe perfyth intellygens' (158–60). Even when Poeta is bold enough to suggest that the play itself has persuasive or didactic power, he then corrects himself:

Thus Saule ys conuertyd, as ye se expres,
. . . .
As Holy Scrypture tellyth whoso lyst to loke þerfore.

Thus we comyte yow all to þe Trynyte,
    Conkludyng thys stacyon as we can or may,
Vnder þe correccyon of them þat letteryd be;
    Howbeyt vnable, as I dare speke or say,
    The compyler hereof shuld translat veray
So holy a story, but wyth fauorable correccyon
Of my honorable masters, of þer benygne supplexion.   (346, 352–9)

The insistence upon the correction of the learned, despite the mixed nature of the audience – 'thys wurshypfull congragacyon,/ That here be present of hye and low degre' (361–2) – suggests that the playwright or 'compyler' of *The Conversion of Saint Paul* did not anticipate only one kind of response from the audience; nor, therefore, could he have anticipated that any of his rhetorical means would have a unified effect. While the playwright anticipates protest from those who are learned, he does not expect it from those who are not.

Anticipation of a mixed response might have been reasonable at the time. The original version of *The Conversion of Saint Paul* – that is, the version that existed before the later additions in the manuscript – seems to have been written at some time in the early 1500s, based upon the watermarks and handwriting; the later additions, including the episode of Belial and Mercury and the various stage directions saying '*Daunce*,' seem to have been made mid-century.[2] These dates would place the original performing lifetime of the play squarely during the decades leading to and following the Act of Supremacy in 1534 that began the English Reformation. During this period, the struggle between the proponents of traditional religion and the proponents of radicalism was not merely political but philosophical; it was a struggle between 'a religion of ceremonial practise [... and] a religion of the word.'[3] It is also true that *The Conversion of Saint Paul* shows, within itself, aspects of both religions; indeed, the entire play shows an uneasy tension between the two.

It would be tempting at this point to draw too large a conclusion, and to declare that *The Conversion of Saint Paul* may be a reformist or even a Protestant play. However, the most that can be said with any certainty is that, under certain hypothetical performative conditions, the play might not have been offensive to some varieties of reformer who may have seen it. Heather Hill-Vasquez, for one, argues that the play 'must have been originally composed and produced to suit Catholic sensibilities' but 'also could be performed to suit an alternative theology.'[4] Certainly the play contains none of the explicit anti-papal rhetoric of, for instance, Bale's *King John*. Even Poeta's insistence on the authority of the Bible cannot be seen as Protestant; as the play's editors note, his recommendation of '*Actum Appostolorum*' seems to be a translation from the Catholic service for matins on the feast of Saint Paul: 'Quod si rebus ipsis id ita fieri videre disideras, lege. Actuum Apostolorum librum, perspicies profecto. But if you desire to see how it was with these things, read the Acts of the Apostles, so that you may understand profitably.'[5] What can be said is that the play is aware of and uneasy about its own project of persuading an audience to holy living. It is aware that its audience is a mixed group, that both verbal and visual rhetorical devices are useful but dangerous, and that it nonetheless is needful to attempt to bring the audience together, to persuade them with all available means to community and faith.

Paul is a singularly appropriate subject for such a play. Paul's epistles, of course, were in general addressed to mixed audiences for the very purpose of persuading them to holy living as communities. They also show, not incidentally, that he was a master of rhetoric;[6] nor was this fact lost on Augustine, who calls Paul 'eloquentem nostrum' (our orator).[7] Those writings also show, however, that Paul saw the usefulness of rhetoric but did not trust it for its own sake. This point of view is made most clear in his writings to the Corinthians: 'et sermo meus, et praedicatio mea non in persuabilibus humanae sapientiae verbis, sed in ostensione Spiritus et virtuti' (my speech and my preaching was not in the persuasive words of human wisdom, but in shewing of the Spirit and power [1 Cor. 2:4]); and 'Ita et vos per linguam nisi manifestum sermonem dederitis: quomodo scietur id quod dicitur?' (Except you utter by the tongue plain speech, how shall it be known what is said? [1 Cor. 14:9]). Paul also stressed the importance of the presence of divine grace in the act of preaching, thus removing the emphasis from human skill and placing it upon the sheer power of God's message[8] and his knowledge of it: 'Et si inperitus sermone, sed non scientia' (For although I be rude in speech, yet not in knowledge [2 Cor. 11:6]).

Not only Paul's own writings but also the commentary of those who came after him stressed these same factors. For example, Augustine asks, 'Quid enim prodest locutionis integritas quam non sequitur intellectus audientis?' (What is the use of correct speech if it does not meet with the listener's understanding?)[9] and Aquinas notes, 'Quod fit dum aliquis sic loquitur quod auditorem flectat [...] Spiritus Sanctus utitur lingua hominis quasi quodam instrumento: ipse autem est qui perficit operationem interius' ([W]hen a man so speaks as to *move* his hearers [...] the Holy Spirit uses the tongue of a man as a sort of instrument; and it is the same spirit which completes the work inwardly).[10] In these comments, and in this attitude, one might sense a rejection of rhetoric altogether; in the Digby play, which is necessarily performative and therefore rhetorical, this attitude translates into the same kind of uneasiness with rhetoric that we have already noted in the Thomas plays, including an acute awareness of both the value and the limits of rhetorical *logos* in the face of mystery.

Paul's own character, the dramatist's primary vehicle for the conveyance of such an attitude, is of course well attested from the New Testament sources: better attested, in some ways, than the character of any of the other figures that we have considered. Stubborn, irascible, passionate, eloquent, Paul's character in the Acts of the Apostles and in his epistles remains in many ways the same in the Digby play, before and after his conversion. Furthermore, the *Legenda aurea*'s account of Paul's conversion lays out aspects of his character with which the Digby playwright seems to have been familiar.[11]

Paulus enim tria uitia in se habebat. Primum erat audacia, quod notatur in hoc quod dicitur: 'Accessit ad principem sacerdotum etc.' Glossa: 'Non uocatus, sed sponte zelo concitante eum.' Secundum erat superbia, quod notatur in hoc quod dicitur 'Spirans minarum etc.' Tertium erat carnalis intellegia quam scilicet in lege habebat.

Paul had three vices, the first being wanton boldness, which he demonstrated by going to the high priests: 'He was not summoned,' says the

Gloss, 'but went on an impulse, driven by his zeal.' His second vice was insolent pride, because he is said to have breathed out threats of violence against the disciples of the Lord. The third was that he understood the Law according to the flesh.[12]

The importance of *ethos* in this play cannot be denied; the playwright's use of Paul rather than another figure, and Poeta's constant reference to the *auctoritas* of the Bible and of those audience members not 'lackyng lyttural scyens' (657), show that the persuasive power of authority and *ethos* is among the foremost of the play's concerns: both proper and improper authority, as in the Digby *Mary Magdalene*, but also the propriety of the use of *ethos* at all in persuading an audience to virtue.

Finally, the play lacks nothing in *pathos*, nor does it fail to use *pathos* to great effect. Like Joseph in the York Cycle, Paul in the Digby play is positioned in multiple roles: tyrant, victim, penitent, preacher, prisoner, member of a company. The audience, which is made to be more directly involved in this than in perhaps any other Middle English play, must both physically and rhetorically reconfigure itself constantly in order to engage with the scenes played before it. In the process of doing so, the audience itself becomes a crucial part of the play, and the play becomes a part of the audience's own world.

In drawing upon these three modes of persuasion, the Digby playwright creates a play that fulfils in miniature the functions of Middle English biblical drama: it teaches, moves, and persuades an audience to follow the experience of Paul sympathetically, and encourages them to use the experience of that following to reconsider their own lives. While in the past three chapters we have focused on one means of persuasion at a time, here let us consider all three, so that we might begin to build up a more complete picture of how the rhetorical function of saintly character works in Middle English biblical drama.

The limits of rhetorical proof are both explored and clarified in *Saint Paul*, in the relationship between visual and verbal signification. The original play (or at least the oldest extant version), without the devils or the dances, moves from the former to the latter as its plot develops, even to the point of describing rather than staging the escape of Paul via basket over the city wall.[13] In its movement, the play explores the relationship between proofs as visual icons of authority and proofs as verbal structures of reason.

In Saul's initial appearance, both the visual and the verbal come forth as indications of his power; the latter kind, however, are ancillary to the former. Of course, the audience will see Saul *'goodly besene in þe best wyse, lyke an aunterous knyth'* (s.d. 13) before he begins to speak, yet what he then says reinforces the visual: 'Most dowtyd man I am lyuyng vpon the ground,/*Goodly besene*, wyth many a ryche garlement!' (14–15, my emphasis). Nor is this incident isolated; even when Saul receives his horse to go on his way, its primary benefit is visual. It too is 'goodly besene' (128), and, the soldier assures Saul, 'wyll spede your mater' (130), which could mean either that the horse will hasten his journey by its speed, or that it will bolster his authority, hence his arguments, by its splendour. These references, a form of what David Mills has called the 'behold and see' convention,[14] are so closely worded to each other that they must be considered part of a unified attempt to make a point about visual significations of power. That point seems to be that a society that depends upon the visual at the expense of the verbal is locating its authority in an unstable place. For example, one of the most striking moments of the play comes when Saul receives his letters of authority from Caiaphas and Annas:

> *Anna.* And by thes letturs þat be most reuerrent,
>   Take them in hand, full agre þerto,
> Constreyne all rebellys by owur hole assent,
>   We gyf yow full power so to doo.
>
> . . . .
> *Her Saule resayuyth ther letters.*
>
> *Saulus.* Thys precept here I take in hande,
>   To fullfyll after yowur wyllys both.   (49–53, s.d. 57–8)

Annas tells Saul to take the letters and agree to them; he does not tell Saul to read the letters, nor is there any indication that Saul does so. The letters exist as a visual icon of Saul's deputized authority, both to the audience and to Saul's fellow characters; they are as much a part of Saul's costume as any other ornament.

The Digby play explores not only Saul's dependence upon the visual but also the irony of such dependence; that irony is rendered plain in the comic scene between the stable boy and Saul's servant. While the dynamics of this scene seem to have much in common with those of the Belial and Mercury scene (indeed, the characters could easily be doubled with each other), the stable boy and Saul's servant do not seem to represent later additions, but to constitute part of the original

Digby play.[15] Much of the comedy of this scene depends upon the stable boy's claim of authority and nobility, based upon a visual icon that came from his master:

> *Stabularyus.* I am non hosteler, nor non hosterlers kynne,
>   But a jentylmanys seruuant, I!
> . . . .
> [*Seruus.*] A seruand ye are, and þat a good!
>   Ther ys no better lokyth owt of a hood!
>
> *Stabularyus.* Forsoth, and a hood I vse for to were,
>   Full well yt ys lynyd wyth sylk and chamlett;
>   Yt kepyth me fro the cold, þat þe wynd doth me not dere,
>   Nowther frost nor snow þat I therby do sett.   (89–90, 111–16)

The stable boy's claims would have seemed ridiculous to a contemporary audience. His silk and camlet hood is far too expensive to have been anything other than a hand-me-down from his master (possibly Saul himself); his statement that it keeps him warm is directly opposed to the kind of thinking about such hand-me-downs that appeared in penitentials, among other places. Chaucer's *Parson's Tale*, for example, asserts, 'if so be that they [the rich] wolde yeven [...] clothyng to the povre folk, it is nat convenient to were for hire estaat, ne suffisant to beete hire necessitee, to kepe hem fro the distemperance of the firmament.'[16] The stable boy's visual signifier of rank, so obviously secondhand and worthless as it is, provides an ironic commentary on Saul's visual signifiers, which are also borrowed and worthless.

The real source of power in the play lies not in visual signals but in the word. As Saul is blown off of his horse, and '*Godhed spekyth in heuyn*' (s.d. 183), Saul is relieved of his sight, and must rely on words alone: 'What woldyst I ded? Tell me here!' (189). Indeed, Saul's primary symbol of authority, his horse, is rendered as ironic as the stable boy's hood by God's line, 'Yt ys hard to pryke agayns þe spore!' (184). While this line is entirely scriptural (Acts 9:5), it is given an ironic twist in the Digby play by the presence of the horse; by God's word Saul's apparent role as rider and commander is overthrown, and he becomes the ridden and commanded. Furthermore, the irony of the stable boy and his poor attempts to show visual authority come back to haunt Saul in this moment, as Servus's jeering words, 'Ye were so begrymlyd and yt had been a sowe!' (105) suddenly apply to Saul, face-down in the dirt before the audience.

The importance of words in the second half of the play grows more crucial as visual spectacle gives way to verbal virtuosity. The play's movement away from the visual becomes most striking at its conclusion, in which the escape of Saul from prison is merely described and not staged, a choice that was by no means a practical necessity. In fact, it is described in a language that only the learned in the audience would fully comprehend:

> *Poeta.* Thus leve we Saule wythin þe cyte,
>   The gatys kep by commandment of Caypha and Anna;
> But the dyscyplys in þe ny3t ouer þe wall truly,
>   As the Bybull sayeth: *'dim[i]serunt eum summitten[te]s in sporta.'*   (649–52)

That the play merely found itself unable to stage this scene is possible but not likely. The Digby playwright had no problem imagining spectacular effects of other kinds. Furthermore, the play exists in the same manuscript as the far more spectacular *Mary Magdalene* (which calls for elevating devices of at least equal complexity), and, if John Coldewey is correct,[17] then it is possible that both plays were staged at the same time at least once. Furthermore, that it is not impossible to stage Paul's escape via basket, even for medieval technology, is shown clearly by the Fleury play's staging of that event: 'Tunc Ministri eant et quaera<n>t Saulum. Quo comperto, Saulus cum Discipulis suis in sporta ab aliquo alto loco, quasi a muro, ad terram demittatur' (Then let the attendants go and search for Saul. When this is discovered, let Saul with his disciples be let down to the ground in a hamper from some high place, as if from a wall [Fleury s.d. 73]).[18] It is true that Paul's escape would be easier to stage indoors than outdoors,[19] but the use of elevating devices in other medieval plays, from the York 'Last Judgement' to the N-Town 'Assumption of the Virgin,' suggests that such technology was both known and used in both kinds of setting. It would appear that the ending of the Digby play, then, is not a result of incapability, but of a deliberate theatrical choice to end with words, to turn the audience over to the Bible rather than to those 'That of retoryk haue non intellygens' (660), and to permit the audience itself to complete the story in their own minds.

The play's use of, and dependence on, language, then, show both a reliance upon the word and an uneasiness with visual display, despite the play's spectacle. The writer of this play seems to wish to rely ultimately on the Bible alone for apodictic proof, yet also uses the techniques of rhetoric to move the audience to such an attitude as well.

If the play's use of, and attitude towards, evidence show a tension between two such extremes, so does the depiction of Saul's character itself. The *ethos* of any biblical character, as we have said elsewhere, does of course exist prior to any dramatic speech made by that character; but the case of the Digby Saul is striking nonetheless, for this is a play about conversion; apparently a profound psychological change should take place in the character. Indeed, the conversion of Paul was often seen in psychological terms even in late medieval England. In many Western biblical illustrations of the scene, for example, the moment of Paul's conversion is depicted in 'a personal, psychological sense, by showing Paul in a trance, fallen to the ground and helpless,' rather than depicting the moment in the more placid and abstract Byzantine fashion. The play, of course, depicts Paul's conversion in similar terms, following the Western pattern in every way: Paul is equestrian rather than pedestrian, the figure of God appears rather than merely the hand of God, and Paul is accompanied by two companions.[20] But what the play does with Saul's character during and following the moment of conversion is surprising.

Previous to his conversion, the Digby Saul is established in a manner similar to that of numerous tyrants in medieval drama: like Herod and Pharaoh in any of the cycle plays, or Caesar in the Digby *Mary Magdalene*, Saul introduces himself with a boasting monologue:

> Most dowtyd man I am lyuyng vpon the ground,
>   Goodly besene, wyth many a riche garlement!
> My pere on lyue I trow ys nott found!
>   Thorow þe world, fro þe oryent to þe occydent,
>   My fame ys best knowyn vndyr þe fyrmament!
> I am most dred of pepull vnyuersall –
> They dare not dysp[l]ease me most noble!
> Saule ys my name – I wyll þat ye notyfy –
>   Whych conspyreth the dyscyplys wyth thretys and menacys.   (14–22)

Saul's alliances with the forces of evil are made plain not only by the content of this speech, but also by its style, which is similar to that of many tyrants' speeches in Middle English drama. His association with such tyrants continues throughout the first half of the play, up to the moment of his conversion. Furthermore, the implications of Saul's character are made clear in Ananias's protest to God. In Acts 9, Ananias says, 'Domine, audivi a multis de viro hoc, quanta mala sanctis tuis fecerit in Hierusalem: et hic habet potestatem a principibus sacerdotum alligandi omnes qui invocant nomen tuum' (Lord, I have heard by many of this man, how much evil he hath done to thy saints in Jerusalem. And here he hath authority from the chief priests to bind all that invoke thy name [Acts 9:13–14]). The play deviates from this simple protest in two ways. First, it focuses more sharply on Ananias's own state of mind; second, it focuses on Saul's personal reputation, not merely on his actions but on his character:

> *Ananias.* Lord, I am aferd, for aluay in my mynd
> I here so myche of hys furyous cruelte,
> Þat for spekyng of þi name to deth he will put me.
>
> . . . .
> Gretly I fere hys cruell tyranny.   (224–6, 246)

Both the character and an appropriate reaction to the character are thus laid before the audience. Ananias's reaction, to be sure, is shown after Saul's blinding, but his reaction is not shown to be unreasonable. Yet God, in speaking to Ananias, suggests that not only have Saul's loyalties been changed, but also Saul himself.

God's words about Saul are not many, but they are suggestive of a significant change in Saul's *ethos*: 'a meke lambe þat a wolf before was namyd' (218). Here and elsewhere, the Digby playwright is closely following the words of Augustine as quoted in the *Legenda aurea*: 'Occisus agnus a lupis fecit agnos de lupis' (The Lamb that was slain by wolves turns a wolf into a lamb).[21] God, accordingly, implies strongly that the change is due solely to his intervention: 'Wyth my stroke of pyte sore ys he paynyde,/Wanting his sygth, for he ys truly blynyde' (222–3). Augustine, as quoted in the *Legenda aurea*, says: 'Prostratus est Paulus ut cecaretur, cecatus est ut mutaretur, mutatus est ut mitteretur, missus est ut pro ueritate pateretur' (Paul was prostrated in order to be blinded, blinded in order to be changed, changed in order to be sent, and sent in order that he might suffer for the truth).[22] Furthermore, both Jacobus and the Digby playwright refer to the moment of conversion as a cure; Jacobus states that Christ healed Paul 'a tumore superbie' (of the tumor of pride),[23] while the Digby playwright's God tells Saul, 'I wyll þe recure!' (187). All of this shows Saul in a moment of profound change in character, which will later be symbolized visually to the audience by a change in costume from knightly garb to 'dyscy-plys wede' (s.d. 502).

The play does, however, show a number of odd features that call into question the exact role of *ethos* in its overall structure. First, although the play is called 'The conuersyon of Seynt Paule' (9), the character does not change his name from Saul to Paul upon his conversion, contrary to popular expectation. In fact, when he is arrested for preaching Christianity, he insists, 'Yes, sertaynly, Saule ys my proper name' (579), thus forgoing a potentially powerful theatrical moment that might have followed the declaration of his new name at this point. Of course, the playwright is being strictly biblical in insisting upon this point: the story of Saul's conversion is told in Acts 9, but the change of name does not occur until Acts 13:9, when the author of Acts quite suddenly refers to 'Saulus autem, qui et Paulus.' 'Saul, otherwise Paul.' Second, the use of a visual change, Saul's change of costume, to signify an ethical change, despite the play's overall movement from the visual to the verbal, may be a kind of reminder or at least an admission that what the audience is seeing is a representation only, and that the figure they are watching is merely a character. The Digby playwright insists, in the realm of *ethos* also, that the Bible is to be the final authority, not the play, oration, or representation based upon it.

The *pathos* of Saul's situation is perhaps the most striking aspect of the play. It is through *pathos* that both the logic of the narrative and the *ethos* of Saul himself are vitalized, and that the audience is able to move towards an understanding of Saul's conversion. Such a perspective on the play's use of *pathos* is not, perhaps, self-evident to a modern reader. The playwright may seem at first to wish to distance the audience from *pathos*, in his use of the narrator Poeta; such a device may be seen as a Brechtian alienation effect. However, Victor I. Scherb has argued convincingly that 'Poeta's speeches mediate between the audience and the action; [...] the dramatist hence partially impels the audience to the proper devotional and intellectual response.'[24] If this is indeed the playwright's strategy (and this book has argued that such was typically the strategy of medieval playwrights), then Poeta cannot be seen as an alienation effect but rather as a rhetorical device emphasizing *pathos*, precisely the opposite of what alienation effects accomplish.

The pathetic elements in *The Conversion of Saint Paul* are many and powerful, but they are encapsulated in the moment of Saul's fall from his horse. As Saul lies upon the *platea* before the audience, he bursts forth in a moment of pure emotion:

> O mercyfull god, what aylyth me?
>   I am lame, my leggys be take me fro!
> My sygth lykwyse, I may nott see!
>   I can nott tell whether to goo!
>   My men hath forsake me also.
> Whether shall I wynde, or whether shall I pas?
> Lord, I beseche the, helpe me of thy grace!   (197–203)

As a description of what is happening to Saul externally, this speech is incorrect in several particulars. It is not true that he is lamed; Scripture specifies, 'Surrexit autem Saulus de terra' (And Saul arose from the ground) ([Acts 9:8]), and moments later he must make his way to the Damascus *locus*. It is also not true that he cannot tell where to go, because God has just told him where: 'Aryse, and goo þou wyth glad chere/ Into the cyte a lytyll besyde' (190–1). Finally, it is not yet true that his men have forsaken him; they are in plain view of the audience, and one of them immediately replies, 'Syr, we be here to help in þi nede' (204). By contrast, the Fleury play remains scriptural by having Saul note only that he is blind: 'Cur me meo priuasti lumine?' (Why have you deprived me of my sight? [Fleury 26]).[25] The Digby speech, then, has as its primary focus not the conveyance of information but the stirring of emotion; just as the specific details of the Crucifixion in the *Meditationes vitae Christi* are there to stir rather than teach the reader,[26] so also the specific (but here transparently ahistorical) details of Saul's plight exist to stir and involve the audience. The purpose here is *movere*, rather than *docere*.

The Conversion of Saint Paul is best known for the way in which it involves its audience directly in its action. Most scholars believe that the audience is expected to move physically with the progress of the play; Mary del Villar disagrees, arguing that the text's mention of procession means instead, 'follow and pay attention with all diligence to the general argument of the play.'[27] Yet there is no reason why Poeta's words should not mean both. Indeed, it is possible to see, in the audience's physical entanglement with the world of the play, the same kind of phenomenon that we have observed in the York Cycle: the audience by implication plays multiple and developing roles in relation to the saint, in such a way as to bring them by sympathy closer to him and to the tradition of faith he represents.

There are two characters mediating between the audience and the play: Poeta and Saul. Poeta appears first, casting the audience in an honorable light, reminding them that Jesus 'for vs sufferd payne' (4), and calling them 'thys wyrshypfull audyens/Honorable frendys' (6–7). He implies also that the audience is to react critically and actively to the play, begging their 'lycens [...] vnder your correccyon [...] wyth yowur fauour' (7, 9, 13). After this polite praise, Saul's appearance may seem somewhat jarring. His declaration that he is 'most drad of pepull vnyuersall' (19) seems to cast the audience as his cowering subjects, in much the same way as does the emperor's boast at the outset of the Digby *Mary Magdalene*. This speech, however, comes after the praise of Poeta, in which the audience is reminded to be critical. The audience at this point may seem to have a choice: whether to imagine itself as one of those subjects, projecting itself into the scene, or whether to hold back. It is possible, perhaps likely, that the audience would be split, some members following one course and some another. At any rate, Saul's first direct address to them, 'Saul ys my name – I wyll þat ye notyfy – /Whych conspyreth the dyscyplys wyth thretys and menacys' (21–2), both invites the audience to take note and, by contrast of the second-person pronoun and the third-person reference to the disciples, invites the audience to separate itself in imagination from those disciples. Furthermore, Saul's statement that 'We wyll them nott suffer to rest in no place' (26) is a further invitation to the audience to decide on its temporary sympathies: with us or with them. Thus, from the outset, a series of choices is given by implication for the audience; how its members are to position themselves is largely up to them.

It is during Saul's journey to Damascus that the most striking choice has to be made. Poeta reappears with more respectful words to the audience, 'Besechyng thys audyens to folow and succede/Wyth all your delygens þis generall processyon' (156–7); however, Poeta also stresses the importance of the audience's involvement emotionally, not merely intellectually, when he advises, 'Take ye good hede, and therto gyf affeccyon!' (168). The term 'affeccyon' here means a strong emotional involvement leading to decision. The term was used by John Trevisa as a synonym for any emotion: 'Affecions ben foure Joye Hope Drede and Sorowe';[28] Chaucer's Parson describes fortitude as 'an affeccioun thurgh which a man despiseth anoyouse thinges.'[29] The audience's emotional involvement is also called upon by Saul, who now speaks of his own emotions regarding his task and his intended victims:

My purpose to damask fully I intende;
    To pursue the dyscypulys, my lyfe I apply!

For to breke down the chyrchys thus I condescende.
  Non I wyll suffer that shall edyfey –
  Perchaunce owur lawes they my3te therby,
And the pepull also, turne and conuerte,
Whych shuld be gret heuynes vnto myn hart.   (169–75)

The audience again has choices: the audience may choose to follow
Saul both physically and emotionally, or may hold back; they may
engage their emotions at this point or not.[30]

The unquestioned need for the audience to become fully engaged
happens at the moment when Saul does so, at the moment of his
encounter with the divine. The appearance of God is curious in this
play; it is possible that one actor only played God in both the appearances to Saul and to Ananias, and indeed the speech headings read
'Deus' in both scenes. It is true, however, that the stage directions refer
to two different aspects of God: during Saul's conversion, it is 'God-
head [that] spekyth in heuyn' (s.d. 182), while a few minutes later it is
'Cryst [who] apperyth to Annanie' (s.d. 210). The difference seems
unlikely to have been a mere slip of the pen, given the precise and not
uncommonly understood differences between the two aspects of God,
as in Margery Kempe's experience when she is forced to compare the
two in a vision: 'Þan þe creatur kept sylens in her sowle & answeryd
not þerto, for sche was ful sor aferd of þe Godhed & sche cowde no
skyll of þe dalyawns of þe Godhede, for al hir lofe & al hir affeccyon
was set in þe manhode of Crist & þerof cowde sche good skylle & sche
wolde for no-thyng a partyd þerfro.'[31] If this same distinction is pre-
served in the iconography of The Conversion of Saint Paul, then the possible reactions to, and understanding of, the appearances to Saul and to
Ananias are more complex and variable than they may appear at first
glance.

The appearance of God to Saul is, in the original version of the play
at least, the most strikingly spectacular of moments. 'Here comyth a
feruent, wyth gret tempest, and Saule faulyth down of hys horse; þat
done, Godhed spekyth in heuyn' (s.d. 182), read the stage directions.
The spectacle, as we have seen, is not accompanied by strictly biblical
details: the laming of Saul, for example, is not mentioned in Acts. Furthermore, the words of Deus in the Digby play are not exactly biblical
either. While they do contain the strictly scriptural but rather odd
phrase 'Yt ys hard to pryke agayns the spore!' (184),[32] they nonetheless
change perhaps the most crucial word in the scene. Instead of saying,

'Ego sum Iesus, quem tu persequeris' (I am Jesus whom thou persecut-
est' [Acts 9:5]), the Digby playwright's God says,

> I am þi Savyour þat ys so trwe,
>> Whych made heuyn and erth, and eche creature.
>> Offende nott my goodnes; I wyll þe recure!   (185–7)

In this version of God's appearance to Saul, the majesty rather than the
humanity of God is stressed. Such emphasis is reinforced in God's
directions to Saul; instead of telling him simply, 'Surge, et ingredere
civitatem, et dicetur tibi quid te oporteat facere' (Arise and go into the
city; and there it shall be told thee what thou must do [Acts 9:7]), the
Digby playwright's God elaborates greatly, showing the extent to
which he is responsible for all that will happen to Saul:

> Aryse, and goo þou wyth glad chere
>> Into the cyte a lytyll besyde,
> And I shall þe socor in euery dere,
>> That no maner of yll xal betyde,
>> And I wyll ther for the prouyde
> By my grete goodnes what þou shalt doo.
> Hy þe as fast thether as þou mast goo.   (190–6)

Of course, the Digby playwright must elaborate upon every aspect of
the account in Acts if he does not wish his play to end after a few minutes; but the precise choice of emphasis in elaboration is quite particular in this scene. It is also rather different from the emphasis in God's
appearance to Ananias.

In the latter scene, the playwright has slightly different material to
work from, because the account in Acts takes the form of a dialogue.
The biblical Ananias protests to God, implying that going to Saul
would endanger his own life; God replies merely, 'Vade, quoniam vas
electionis est mihi iste, ut portet nomen meum coram gentibus, et regi-
bus, et filiis Israhel. Ego enim ostendam illi quanta oporteat eum pro
nomine meo pati' (Go thy way: for this man is to me a vessel of elec-
tion, to carry my name before the gentiles and kings and the children
of Israel. For I will shew him how great things he must suffer for my
name's sake [Acts 9:15–16]). In the Digby play, this statement is
expanded into a rather personal exchange between God and Ananias,
in which Ananias speaks of his fear of Saul and in which God urges his

disciple, 'Do my behest! Be nothyng ashamyd!' (219), and 'Nay, Ananie, nay, I assure þe,/He wulbe glad of thy cummyng!' (227–8), and 'Be nothyng a-drad! He ys a chosen wessell [...] A very pynacle of þe fayth, I ensure the' (234, 240), and 'Be nothyng in dowte for good nor yll./Farewell, Ananie! Tell Saule what I do say' (243–4). In this exchange, the playwright's emphasis is entirely different from that in the exchange between Saul and God. Whereas the earlier exchange emphasizes God's grandeur, even to the point of not using the name of Jesus, the later exchange emphasizes God's humaneness even when the original text does not.

Of course, the difference between these two exchanges is the audience to whom God addresses himself. Saul is yet 'a wolf [...] truly blynde' (218, 223), while Ananias is a leader of the disciples; it is natural that a speaker would address himself differently to a different audience. Yet the play's audience witnesses both exchanges, and the strategy directed at them is complex. The audience watching the scene of Saul's conversion has two figures before them: a powerful representation of God, and a powerless and pathetic representation of Saul, lying upon the ground and speaking of his helplessness. The same audience watching God's conversation with Ananias sees a quite different relationship: one in which the disciple may ask questions, even protest, but will still obey without needing rebuke, and in which God remains omnipotent but is also reassuring, even avuncular. It may be simplistic to see the difference as that between a stereotypically Old Testament God and a stereotypically New Testament God, but it is certain that a difference along those lines is being represented.

A guide to the audience's response may be found in an unlikely place: the dialogue between the two soldiers that separates Ananias's conversation with God from his meeting with Saul. The fourteen-line exchange between the two seems a throwaway scene, meant primarily to provide covering dialogue while the actor playing 'Ananias goth toward Saule' (s.d. 247). However, the playwright again changes and expands upon the scriptural details of his source in specific and telling ways in this scene.

The accounts of Saul's companions in Acts are unspecific and inconsistent, saying that they 'stabant stupefacti, audientes quidem vocem, neminem autem videntes' (stood amazed, hearing indeed a voice but seeing no man [Acts 9:7]), or, alternately, that they 'lumen quidem viderunt: vocem autem non audierunt eius, qui loquebatur' (saw indeed the light: but they heard not the voice of him that spoke) [Acts

22:9]). The Digby playwright, however, expands these notes into a brief but detailed dialogue:

Primus Myles. I maruayle gretly what yt doth mene,
    To se owur master in thys hard stounde!
The wonder grett lythys þat were so shene
    Smett hym doune of hys hors to þe grownde,
    And me thowt that I hard a sounde
Of won spekyng wyth voyce delectable,
Whych was to [vs] wonderfull myrable.

Secundus Myles. Sertenly thys lyȝt was ferefull to see,
    Ther sperkys of fyer were very feruent!
Yt inflamyd so greuosely about þe countre,
    That, by my trowth, I went we shuld a bene brent!
    But now, serys, lett vs relente
Agayne to Caypha and Anna to tell þis chaunce,
How yt befell to vs thys greuauns.   (248–61)

The first soldier in this account heard a voice though no specific words, 'a sounde/Of won spekyng' (252–3) only; the second does not seem to have heard a voice at all but saw only the fire; one soldier comes (roughly) from 9:7, and the other (roughly) from 26:9. For a moment, the two soldiers are suspended between two worlds. The first soldier concentrates on their master and on the 'wonderfull myrable' (254) of the speaking voice that he has heard, though he does so uncomprehendingly. The second, however, admits grudgingly only that the visual evidence of the event was 'ferefull,' 'very feruent,' and a 'greuauns' (255–6, 261). Furthermore, they are not speaking only to each other, but to the audience; the second soldier says not 'ser' but 'serys' (259), and invites the audience to return with him to the high priests, to the world of visual icons of power, and to incomprehension of the event they have witnessed.

Yet the play continues not with the priests but at the Damascus *locus*. It seems certain that the audience is meant to remain with Saul, not to return to Caiaphas and Annas either physically or sympathetically, and are to be witnesses to Saul's joy at being healed and baptized and to the appearance of the Holy Spirit over him. And yet, Poeta's exposition of the scene following Saul's conversion is rather blasé, emphasizing the teaching rather than the moving function of the scene:

Poeta. Thus Saule ys conuertyd, as ye se expres,
   The very trw seruant of our Lord Jhesu.
Non may be lyke to hys perfy3t holynes,
    So nobyll a doctor, constant and trwe;
    After hys conuersyon neuer mutable, but styll insue
The lawys of god to teche euer more and more,
As Holy Scrypture tellyth whoso lyst to loke þerfore.

Thus we comyte yow all to þe Trynyte,
   Conkludyng thys stacyon as we can or may,
Vnder þe correccyon of them þat letteryd be;
    Howbeyt vnable, as I dare speke or say,
    The compyler hereof shuld translat veray
So holy a story, but wyth fauorable correccyon
Of my honorable masters, of þer benygne supplexion.   (346–59)

The centre of the play is not, it turns out, Saul's conversion in itself, but the sermon in which Saul preaches to the audience on the Seven Deadly Sins. It is here that the playwright most fully engages the audience, and most vividly shows the nature and purpose of his central character.

This sermon is the play's primary example of extended rhetoric, and thus deserves consideration at some length. It is a complex work of rhetoric in miniature, using all three means of persuasion and numerous strategies. Robert of Basevorn's description of Paul's method of preaching as shown in the epistles is also a fair assessment of the Digby Saul's sermon: 'Paul used reason with great success, especially together with authority – now taking a reason from authority, now conforming reason with authority, now commending the hearers, now saddening them, now flattering them, now disparaging them, now totally committing himself to God, now helping himself with human industry.'[33] All of these techniques, sometimes separately, sometimes combined, can be seen in Paul's sermon.

The play's editors note that the sermon functionally is an illustration of Acts 9:20, 'And immediately he preached Jesus in the synagogues, that he is the Son of God.'[34] The sermon itself does indeed affirm such doctrine, calling Jesus 'owur Sauyour' (544), but in its treatment of the Seven Deadly Sins it also shows a surprising use of scripture as proof. As we have noted, the real Paul often used scripture as apodeictic proof; so does the Digby Saul, but with a difference. In the Pauline epistles, the Old Testament is quoted in the Greek of the Septuagint, the same language in which Paul wrote and presumably in which the recipients of the epistles read and conversed; the Digby Saul, on the other hand, quotes Scripture in the Latin of the Vulgate, and does not always translate it. Three examples show the effects that this practice has; in the first, Saul provides a translation before introducing the quotation itself:

> Pryde, þat of bytternes all bale begynnes,
>> Wythholdyng all fayth, yt fedyth and foysonnys,
> As Holy Scrypture baryth playn wytnes:
>> '*Initium omnium peccatorum su[per]bia est*' –
> That often dystroyth both man and best.   (511–15)

In the second example, Saul translates the quotation after introducing it:

> For Pryde and hys progeny mekenes confoundys.
>> '*Quanto maior es tanto humilia te in omnibus*' –
> The gretter þou art, the lower loke thu be;
>> Bere the neuer þe hyer for þi degre.   (547–50)

Finally, in this passage Saul does not directly translate the quotation at all:

> Off all vyces and foly, pryde ys the roote;
>> Humylyte may not rayn ner yet indure.
> Pyte, alak, that ys flower and boot,
>> Ys exylyd wher pryde hath socour.
>> '*Omnis qui se exaltat humiliabitur.*'
> Good Lord, gyf vs grace to vnderstond and perseuer,
> Thys wurd, as þou bydyst, to fulfyll euer.   (516–22)

Effectively, Saul's sermon treats the Latin Scriptures as proof in two different ways. Not only does he cite them as the sources of his advice, but he also uses the language itself as a kind of verbal icon. Eamon Duffy notes[35] that even many of the unlettered would have had some oral comprehension of Latin, although that comprehension may have been limited to the recognition that Latin was now being spoken, and that the Latin was the text upon which the sermon was based. In this sense, to the unlettered members of the audience particularly, quotations are similar in effect to his closed letters of authority: opaque verbal icons. The key differences, of course, are that Saul's icons now derive from God rather than from earthly powers, and that they are verbal rather than visual, but the dynamic is similar.[36] Saul uses them to indicate the authority of his teaching, and to indicate that that source is the God of his audience's own community: the church.

The sermon itself, furthermore, is an elaborate though understated example of rhetoric in its own right. Its understanding of its implied audience, its line of argument, and its figures of thought and speech represent a distillation of many of the issues of saintly rhetoric that medieval playwrights explored.

The audience, Saul notes immediately, is certainly a mixed lot. In his wish that God should 'Save þis asemly þat here syttyth or stond' (504), he acknowledges the varying levels of class, education, and wealth in the audience, as Mercy does in *Mankind*.[37] Yet he also, unlike Mercy the daughter of God, identifies himself with that mixed lot, by continuing, 'For hys meke mercy, þat we do not spyll' (505). Having established that the audience consists of 'Welbelovyd fryndys' (509), he launches into an exposition of the Seven Deadly Sins.

Saul's sermon emphasizes two particular sins: pride and lust.[38] Saul's pride, of course, was manifest to the audience from the moment of his initial appearance; his lust is suggested by his statement upon conversion, 'For my offencys, my body shal haue punycyon' (303).[39] The lust that Saul seems to be primarily guilty of, however, is not sexual lust, but rather the kind of thinking that places the law higher than grace:

Nam quod inpossible erat legis, in quo infirmabatur per carnem: Deus Filium suum mittens in similitudinem carnis peccati et de peccato, damnavit peccatum in carne, ut iustificatio legis impleretur in nobis, qui non secundum carnem ambulamus, sed secundum spiritum.

For what the law could not do, in that it was weak through the flesh, God, sending his own Son in the likeness of sinful flesh and of sin, hath condemned sin in the flesh. That the justification of the law might be fulfilled in us who walk not according to the flesh, but according to the spirit.

(Rom 8:3–4)

Saul's sermon thus makes the audience reflect not only upon the *ethos* of the man they see before them, but also upon the *ethos* of the man as he was before his conversion. Indeed, the character of Paul, like Augustine in the *Confessions*, 'does not discredit his past experience but rather actively incorporates it in a sense of guilt and illumination of the present with the memory of past habits.'[40] Furthermore, in bringing Saul down upon the *platea* to preach the sermon, as the play surely does, the playwright identifies the audience with the early Christian community, Saul's original audience. Thus the play grounds its audience's identity as Christians in centuries of history as well as in doctrinal teaching. Furthermore, far from a merely intellectual treatment of the Seven Deadly Sins, Saul's description of them is rendered immediate and personal by his identification with, and of, the audience; when, for instance, he notes that pride 'often dystroyeth both most and lest,'[41] he recalls his earlier characterization of the audience and urges them to consider the sin in their own lives.

Saul does not only rely on authority, and on identifying himself with the audience, however. He also reasons with his audience, inviting them to follow an intellectual argument. For instance, the fourth stanza takes the form of a kind of enthymeme;

> Whoso in pryde beryth hym to hye,
>> Wyth mysheff shalbe mekyd as I mak mensyon.
> And I therfor assent and fully certyfy
>> In text, as I tell the trw entencyon
>> Of perfy3t goodnes and very locucyon:
> *'Noli tibi dico in altum sapere sed time.'*
> Thys ys my consell: bere the not to hye!   (523–9)

One could rewrite the stanza almost as a syllogism: All those who are proud will come to grief; therefore (if you wish to be saved) do not be one of the proud. The unspoken assumption, that the audience wishes to be saved, clearly identifies the sermon as one that takes place before the Christian community; in addition, the use of the scriptural quotation as the conclusion, not premise, of the argument shows that Saul expects the audience to realize that reason and revelation are not at odds with each other: in short, that they as Christians have the responsibility and the capacity to think and to make moral decisions.

By comparing the sermon to Saul's opening boast, one can see the change in Saul's character that has taken place. Not only is the genre of the speech different – a recognizably homiletic speech rather than a tyrannical one – but so also is its style. Though the verse form remains the same, the language has become macaronic, and, strangely, more alliterative. Such lines as 'Saue þis asemly þat here syttyth or stond' (504) and 'Whych be provyd pryncypall and pryncys of poysons' (510) have no precedent in any of Saul's prior speeches. Such sudden opacity of speech might be the opposite of what one might expect, but as Jeanette Dillon has shown,[42] medieval plays were by no means of a piece in their treatment of rhetorical opacity.[43] In its equation of Latinity and ornateness with holiness, *The Conversion of Saint Paul* is in line with much other East Anglian drama, including the N-Town cycle and *The Castle of Perseverence*, though not with, for instance, the non-East Anglian Towneley cycle, whose Latin/English dialectic is somewhat different.[44] At any rate, the sudden change in Saul's very manner of speaking suggests the depth of the change in him, as does, perhaps, the moment of ambiguity when Saul says, '"Lern at myself, for I am meke in hart" – /Owur Lorde to hys seruantys thus he sayth' (537–8). For a moment it seems as if Saul is speaking of himself, even boasting, yet his attribution of the quotation to God forces the audience to redirect its understanding that it was not Saul talking on his own account: 'Non ego, [...] vero in me Christus' (not I, but Christ [...] in me [Gal. 2:20]). The conversion of Saul is internal, sudden, and thorough;[45] his authority lies in his humility and in his use of the Bible.

The sermon's rhetorical characteristics may at first glance seem somewhat obscured by the structure of the play as it now stands; coming after the interpolated scene between Belial and Mercury, with its visual and verbal pyrotechnics, Saul's sermon may seem drab by comparison. The devils' scene, indeed, necessitates several challenges of performance, none of which is merely technical in nature. The first challenge consists in the visible presence of Annas and Caiaphas. Immediately before the inserted scene, the two high priests are visible to the audience while they discuss what to do with the newly converted Saul; indeed, the devils' discussion merely extends the same topic further. There is no apparent break before Belial's entrance, nor, thematically, does it seem that there should be. Most likely, Annas and Caiaphas must remain visible to the audience for the duration of the devils' scene, and indeed for Saul's sermon that follows. A second challenge is the abrupt shift in tone when switching from the devils to Saul. In the original play, the change in tone need not have been quite so extreme. Annas and Caiaphas are rather restrained in their language as Middle English dramatic villains go; compared to, say, the Coventry Herod or the Towneley Caiaphas, they seem quite civilized, even

Paul and the Rhetoric of Sainthood 103

urbane. Belial and Mercury, by contrast, rant and roar like the worst tyrants of the cycle plays, rendering the contrast with Saul's sermon far more extreme than in the original text.

Annas and Caiaphas's continued visibility actually strengthens one of the basic contrasts made in the original play: that between the visual and the verbal. As Belial appears *'wyth thunder and fyre'* (s.d. 412), shouting, 'beholde me' (413), he calls attention to the visual. When the play is staged, the devils call attention not only to their own appearance but also to the visual aspects of the society of the high priests, even turning the priests themselves into icons:

My busshopys, thorow my motyon, þei wyl hym sone devoure!

I haue movyd my prelatys, Cayphas and Anna,
  To persew and put downe by powre ryall,
Thorow þe sytyes of Damaske and Liba,
  All soch as do worship þe hye God supernall.
  There deth ys conspyryd wythowt any fauoure at all;
My busshopys hathe chosyne won most rygorus
Them to persew, howse name ys *Saulus.*   (418–25)

In this speech, and in the following exchange with Mercury, who suggests that the devils should 'Go to þe busshopys and moue þem pryvelye' (478), the two 'busshopys' are surely still visible to the audience, though unmoving. In an ironic reversal of expectation, the devils or false gods refer, probably by gesture, to the two unmoving priests as the solution to their problem.[46] Annas and Caiaphas seem to have turned into icons, just as Saul's letter from them was an icon. Furthermore, Annas and Caiaphas may also be present during Saul's sermon, metaphorically established in the audience's sight as unmoving, wordless idols, in sharp contrast to Saul's preaching of the Word.

The second of the two challenges, the abrupt shift in tone, also reinforces the original play's strategies. If the priests exemplify the mute stillness of an idol then the devils exemplify the 'unstable, restless, and dissonant' nature of evil, and provide a striking contrast to the 'stable, tranquil, and harmonious'[47] preaching of Paul. Indeed, the devils' scene makes such a contrast more strongly than any part of the original play, and may even correct a possible misunderstanding. While the original play moves its central character from bluster to stillness, it also connects a great deal of spectacle and noise with the appearance of

God. To be sure, the playwright seems to have tried not to make that connection overly strong; the stage direction reads, 'Here comyth a fer- uent, wyth gret tempest, and Saule faulyth down of hys horse'; only when 'þat [is] done' does the action indicate that 'Godhed spekyth in heuyn' (s.d. 183). Still, the moment passes quickly and in performance the separate actions do seem to be one action. It is perhaps for this rea- son that the revisers of the play included such insistently pyrotechnic devils; if God creates one explosion, the devils create three: 'thunder and fyre' (s.d. 412) for Belial's entrance, 'a fyeryng' (s.d. 433) for Mer- cury's entrance, and 'a fyrye flame, and a tempest' (s.d. 502) for their joint exit. Furthermore, the devils' dialogue is marked by such inartic- ulate noises as 'Ho, ho' (412), 'Ho!' (426), 'Ho! Owȝt, owȝt!' (433), 'Ho' (440), 'Ho! Owȝt, owȝt!' (454), 'Ho! Owȝt, owȝt!' (466), 'Owȝt!' (471), and 'Ho' (483), and the stage directions specify that Mercury shall enter 'cryeng and roryng' (s.d. 433) and that they both 'shall rore and crye' (s.d. 471). The two are not merely spectacular and noisy but also anti-verbal.

Heather Hill-Vasquez argues rightly that this 'small interpolated scene [...] can encourage interpretive alterations to the play that extend beyond the scene's boundaries.'[48] However, as she also concedes, the devils' scene is not necessarily reformist, but could easily be a rein- forcement of the play's previous attitudes and strategies.[49] In fact, the overall argument that Hill-Vasquez makes for the allegedly reforming purpose of the devils' scene is unlikely to be true. It is predicated first on the possibility that the devils were costumed in ecclesiastical vest- ments, a contention for which the text of the play provides no support; and second on the extremely unlikely possibility that these two devils, who are entirely open with the audience about their evil purposes, might somehow be able to 'mislead the audience spiritually' and seduce them into 'a beguiling trap' of false religion,[50] thus allowing Saul to reconvert the audience through his sermon. But these are not smooth and eloquent Miltonian devils, and it is a mistake to read them as such.[51]

One cannot finally say for sure that the Digby *Conversion of Saint Paul* is Catholic, Protestant, proto-Protestant, reactionary, or reformist. But certain features of the play are clear: its use of the visual is both spectacular and self-critical; its caution about rhetoric and the use of *logos* in the face of mystery is balanced with its emphasis on the need for persuasive words; its powerful use of *pathos* echoes that of other Middle English playwrights' treatment of saints, while its use of *ethos* in establishing the character of Paul provides a figure who is unambiguously scriptural and insistently textual.

In the end, *The Conversion of Saint Paul* is a complex study in the difficulties and ambiguities of using rhetorical and theatrical techniques to convey divine mysteries through the person of a saint. That it can be seen to have elements of both the medieval way of looking at the saints, through the lens of 'solidarity through suffering'[52] and the newer way of seeing them as 'clarifying the nature of the Word'[53] reflects, to be sure, a tension between two ways of being religious; but the Digby playwright and his revisers seem to have been concerned overall with the audience's immediate experience of the play, of the word, and of the person of Saul. As such, they create and revise a saint play that, like the others we have seen, leads its audience imaginatively from a position of potential doubt to a position of faith logically, ethically, and sympathetically.

6

Conclusion

T.S. Eliot's Magus reports that when he found the Christ child in Bethlehem, 'it was (you may say) satisfactory' (31).[1] Eliot's Magus and his companions find it easier, even after their long, hard journey, to remain in unbelief than to move into a position of faith. They find it easier to remain 'in the old dispensation,/With an alien people clutching their gods' (41–2) than to embrace a new dispensation, even though they know they are 'no longer at ease' (41) and never again can be. Furthermore, the Magus's apostrophe to the readers indicates that he expects at least some of them to recognize the feeling.

Of course, Eliot's 'Journey of the Magi' is a modern poem, and to a medieval audience it may have been an almost inconceivable one. Perhaps more understandable in any era, however, is the less well-known poem that follows it in *Ariel Poems*, 'A Song for Simeon,' in which the old prophet declares, 'Not for me the martyrdom, the ecstasy of thought and prayer,/Not for me the ultimate vision./Grant me thy peace' (29–31).[2] In any era, faith and its implications are difficult.

Perhaps writers in the European Christian tradition have always known this to be true, and have often turned to the persuasive arts as a result. Milton, for example, seems to use rhetoric as a weapon to assail the reader's conscience and unbelief. In his influential book on Milton, *Surprised by Sin*, Stanley Fish argues that 'logic is a safeguard against a rhetorical effect only after the effect has been noted [...] [T]here is no adequate defense against eloquence at the moment of impact.'[3] While Fish's understanding of rhetoric is brutally put (and perhaps that is appropriate for a study of Milton), it describes well both the instantaneously and the continuously manipulative effects that rhetoric can have on a reader or an audience. It does not, however, give that reader or audience much credit, for it does not allow for the possibility that a reader or audience might, in fact, have the time and ability to make decisions, and to acknowledge choices and sympathies. In short, it makes no distinction between persuasion, in which the audience freely assents,[4] and coercion, in which it has no choice but to assent – or is led to believe that it has no choice.

Certainly, the choices that an audience makes in experiencing Middle English biblical drama are, in some ways, predetermined for them; certainly, the rhetoric of the medieval playwrights has 'moments of impact' upon the audience, moments that require decisions and responses; certainly, the plays compel, or try to compel, the audience. Yet the playwrights were aware of the dangerous nature of their tool. They were aware that rhetoric's 'fine phrases' may 'flatter the desires of the cupidinous self'[5] and often worked to show its limits, that rhetoric is in itself a morally neutral instrument that 'et vera suadeantur et falsa (is used to give conviction to both truth and falsehood).'[6] The importance of grounding the audience's experience in the commonality of the Church became paramount, so that private interpretation did not veer into the heretical.

The playwrights, in an attempt to control the ethical orientation of their tools, thus associated some of their most subtle rhetorical effects with holy figures, such as those of the saints, often concentrating on the appeal of *ethos* and, especially, *pathos*. Though these are often thought of as the disreputable species of argument, the medieval playwrights knew both their power and their utility in the arena of faith. To argue by *logos* alone may end up in mere intellectualism, the sort of aridity that Augustine warned against.[7] But the character of a saint and the appeal that such a character can make to the emotions of an audience may not only avoid aridity but also bring about 'the enormous didactic and imaginative effectiveness of the religious plays of the late Middle Ages: once seen, never forgotten.'[8] By co-opting the tools of rhetoric to the side of the saintly, the medieval playwrights created a tool to move the audience to holy living.

Indeed, the flawed humanity of the four saints of this study shows that the playwrights who portrayed them recognized and acknowledged the limitations not only of their art in portraying perfection, but of humanity in achieving it. Thomas, Mary Magdalene, Joseph, and Paul have the common feature of existing at liminal spaces between faith and doubt, a space that all humanity surely inhabits to some degree. In the figures of these saints, a medieval audience may have found not only role models but also means of bringing the power of the divine into their own lives, as individuals and as a community. The audience, in following Paul, Joseph, or Mary Magdalene around the playing space, or even in following Thomas's intellectual doubts, may be as imperfect as they, but the sanctity of those they follow suggests that imperfection may not be an obstacle to the sacred. As Auden wrote, 'To choose what is difficult all one's days/As if it were easy, that is faith. Joseph, praise.'[9] Indeed, the miraculous intervention of God into these saints' lives are salient reminders of divine power, mercy, and compassion: a compassion that the audience also is invited to feel for the flawed, struggling saints in its midst, and for each other by extension.

Ultimately, the rhetoric of the saints attempts to appeal to the audience's better nature, and to bring the audience, as a community, to faith by consent. Not merely teaching, not even merely delighting the audience with affective experiences, the saints in medieval biblical plays achieve sympathy, consent, and solidarity among the faithful. They help the audience understand its role as part of salvation history, and most of all, they bring the audience, through identification, sympathy, and the need for interpretation, to an understanding of themselves as community.

Notes

The following abbreviations are used in the Notes:

DAI	*Dissertation Abstracts International*
EDAM	Early Drama, Art, and Music
EETS es	Early English Text Society, Extra Series
EETS os	Early English Text Society, Old Series
EETS ss	Early English Text Society, Supplementary Series
LCL	Loeb Classical Library
MED	*Middle English Dictionary*
METh	*Medieval English Theatre*
OED	*Oxford English Dictionary*, 2nd ed.
PL	*Patrologia Latina*, ed J.-P. Migne
REED	*Records of Early English Drama*
RORD	*Research Opportunities in Renaissance Drama*

1. Medieval Drama and Community Identity

1 References to the York Cycle are to *The York Plays*, ed. Richard Beadle (London 1982).
2 *Dives and Pauper*, ed. Priscilla Heath Barnum, EETS os 275 (1976), 94.
3 *A Tretise of Miraclis Pleyinge*, ed. Clifford Davidson, EDAM 19 (Kalamazoo 1993), 98. But see Lawrence M. Clopper, '*Communitas*: The Play of Saints in Late Medieval England,' *Mediaevalia* 18 (1995), 81–110, and Clopper, '*Miracula* and *The Tretise of Miraclis Pleyinge*,' *Speculum* 65 (1990), 878–905, for an important *caveat* regarding the nature of 'miraclis.'
4 *REED: York*, ed. Alexandra F. Johnston and Margaret Rogerson (Toronto 1979), ɪ:11, and ɪɪ:697.

5 *REED: Chester*, ed. Lawrence M. Clopper (Toronto 1979), 27.

6 Eamon Duffy, *The Stripping of the Altars: Traditional Religion in England 1400–1580* (New Haven 1992), 131.

7 As Laurelle Marie LeVert puts it, medieval pietistic texts 'are constructed to suggest that one's response defines the meaning of the text, but only when that response is within the bounds of theological orthodoxy.' 'The Rhetoric of Response: Affectivity and Didacticism in Middle English Devotional Experiences of the Passion,' PhD diss., University of Toronto 1999, 12. See also Charles Phythian-Adams, 'Ceremony and the Citizen: The Communal Year at Coventry, 1450–1550,' in *Crisis and Order in English Towns*, ed. Peter Clark and Paul Slack (Toronto 1972), 57–85.

8 Arnold Buchheimer, 'The Development of Ideas About Empathy,' *Journal of Counseling Psychology* 10, no. 1 (1963), 63.

9 *Nicholas Love's Mirror of the Blessed Life of Jesus Christ*, ed. Michael G. Sargent (New York 1992), 47.

10 *The Book of Margery Kempe*, ed. Sanford Brown Meech and Hope Emily Allen, EETS os 212 (London 1940), 19.

11 *A Book of Showings to the Anchoress Julian of Norwich*, ed. Edmund College and James Walsh (Toronto 1978), ii:201–2.

12 *De doctrina Christiana*, 4.2.3, ed. and trans. R.P.H. Green (Oxford 1995), 198–9.

13 A complete list of studies that focus on the villainous or lurid would be enormous. Nonetheless, we may see the scope of the problem by remembering such comments as Owst's 'So much, then, for the development of human character in the miracle-plays' after a six-page treatment of Cain, Noah's wife, Herod and his soldiers, Pilate, Caiaphas, and Annas, with a brief glance at Isaac in *Literature and Pulpit in Medieval England*, 2nd ed. (Oxford 1961), 491–7; or by recalling the fact that the only book by a major scholar on a single character in the drama remains Arnold Williams's *The Characterization of Pilate in the Towneley Cycle* (East Lansing 1950). Other examples include Lysander W. Cushman, *The Devil and the Vice in English Dramatic Literature before Shakespeare* (Halle 1900); Robert A. Brawer, 'The Characterization of Pilate in the York Cycle Play,' *Studies in Philology* 69 (1972), 289–303; David Staines, 'To Out-Herod Herod: The Development of a Dramatic Character,' *Comparative Drama* 10 (1976), 29–53; Miriam Anne Skey, 'Herod the Great in Medieval European Drama,' *Comparative Drama* 13 (1979), 330–64; Lawrence M. Clopper, 'Tyrants and Villains: Characterization in the Passion Sequences of the English Cycle Plays,' *Modern Language Quarterly* 41 (1980), 3–20; Martin Stevens, 'Herod as Carnival King in the Medieval Biblical Drama,' *Mediaevalia* 18 (1995), 43–66; Joseph M. Ricke,

'Parody, Performance, and the "Ultimate" Meaning of Noah's Shrew,' *Mediaevalia* 18 (1995), 263–82; and Jody Enders, *The Medieval Theater of Cruelty: Rhetoric, Memory, Violence* (Ithaca 1999). While these are all excellent and valuable studies, they present only part of the experience of medieval plays.

14 As in, for instance, Heather Hill-Vasquez, 'The Possibilities of Performance: A Reformation Sponsorship for the Digby *Conversion of Saint Paul*,' *REED Newsletter*, 22, no. 1 (1997), 2–20.

15 As in David Mills, 'Characterisation in the English Mystery Plays: A Critical Prologue,' *METh* 5 (1983), 5–17; Garrett P.J. Epp, 'Visible Words: The York Plays, Brecht, and Gestic Writing,' *Comparative Drama* 24 (1990–1), 289–305; Martin Stevens, 'Illusion and Reality in the Medieval Drama,' *College English* 32 (1971), 448–64; Sarah Carpenter, 'Morality-Play Characters,' *METh* 5 (1983), 18–28.

16 As, classically, in E.K. Chambers, *The Mediaeval Stage* (Oxford 1903), ii:209.

17 V.A. Kolve, *The Play Called Corpus Christi* (London 1966), 237–64.

2. Thomas and the Limits of Rhetoric

1 Latin biblical quotations are from the Vulgate, English ones from the Douai version. I have silently regularized the capitalization and punctuation of the *Biblia Sacra iuxta vulgatam versionem*, ed. B. Fischer et al., 4th ed. (Stuttgart, 1994) to match that of the Douai.

2 Gail McMurray Gibson, *The Theater of Devotion: East Anglian Drama and Society in the Late Middle Ages* (Chicago 1989), 16–18.

3 One thinks of Johan Huizinga's assertion that late medieval depictions of death were merely 'superficial, primitive, popular, and lapidary image[s]. [...] It seems as if the late medieval mind could see no other aspect of death than that of decay.' *The Autumn of the Middle Ages* [*Herfsttij der Middeleeuwen* (1921)], trans. Rodney J. Payton and Ulrich Mammitzsch (Chicago 1996), 156.

4 Duffy, *Stripping of the Altars*, 307.

5 Aristotle, *Rhetoric* 1355b–1356a, trans. W. Rhys Roberts, *The Works of Aristotle*, ed. W.D. Ross (Chicago 1952), 595.

6 Eleanor Prosser, *Drama and Religion in the English Mystery Plays: A Reevaluation* (Stanford 1961), 157.

7 All citations of the Towneley Plays, unless otherwise indicated, refer to *The Towneley Plays*, ed. Martin Stevens and A.C. Cawley, EETS ss 13–14 (Oxford 1994), and are cited by play number and line number.

8 It is to be noted that he is never revealed by name to the audience as Paul; only Peter and Thomas are named in the dialogue.

9 Stevens and Cawley, *Towneley Plays* II:618.

10 Rosemary Woolf, *The English Mystery Plays* (London 1972), 282.

11 Ibid., 177.

12 James J. Murphy, *Rhetoric in the Middle Ages: A History of Rhetorical Theory from Saint Augustine to the Renaissance* (Berkeley 1974), 293–6.

13 Henrik Specht, '"Ethopoeia" or Impersonation: A Neglected Species of Medieval Characterization,' *Chaucer Review* 21 (1986), 5.

14 This moment is rather curious, because Thomas then suggests for the first and only time that it may have been an animated corpse that appeared to the apostles: 'It was his cors that maide shewyng/Vnto you in his sted' (Towneley 28/355–6). Such a unique and illogical moment makes one wonder if the scribe mistakenly wrote 'cors' for 'gost,' carrying the word 'cors' over from the previous line, especially since 'Quintus Apostolus' in the next stanza makes a conscious and precise distinction between what Christ's 'gost' did and what his 'cors' did during the period of his death, as if answering a point of Thomas's. Chester N. Scoville, 'A Scribal Error in Towneley Play 28,' *Notes and Queries* New Series 47.3 (September 2000), 298–9.

15 Richard A. Lanham, *A Handlist of Rhetorical Terms*, 2nd ed. (Berkeley 1991), 166.

16 Gerald A. Hauser, *Introduction to Rhetorical Theory* (Prospect Heights 1986), 72.

17 Woolf notes (*English Mystery Plays*, 283) that it is influenced by the affective mystical school of Richard Rolle.

18 Duffy, *Stripping of the Altars*, 307.

19 *The N-Town Play*, ed. Stephen Spector, EETS ss 11–12 (Oxford 1991).

20 See *The Passion Play from the N.Town Manuscript*, ed. Peter Meredith (London 1990), and Spector, *N-Town Play*, II:537–43.

21 Spector, *N-Town Play*, II:560.

22 E. Catherine Dunn, 'The Literary Style of the Towneley Plays,' *American Benedictine Review* 20 (1969), 483.

23 It is possible that the episode appeared in some form in the Towneley and Chester cycles. The former cycle seems to be missing some form of Marian play, the removal of which accounts for the missing first page of the 'Judgment' play; the latter cycle is certainly missing a play of the Assumption, though we have no information on its exact scope. See Martin Stevens, 'The Missing Parts of the Towneley Cycle,' *Speculum*, 45 (1970), 254–65, and *REED: Chester*, ed. Clopper, 20, 23–4, 37–8.

24 Marina Warner, *Alone of All Her Sex: The Myth and the Cult of the Virgin Mary* (New York 1983), 278.
25 See Carolyn Wall, 'The Apocryphal and Historical Backgrounds of "The Appearance of Our Lady to Thomas" (Play XLVI of the York Cycle),' *Mediaeval Studies*, 32 (1970), 172–92.
26 Jacobus de Voragine [Iacopo da Varazze], *Legenda Aurea*, ed. Giovanni Paolo Maggioni (Sismel 1998), ii:786; *The Golden Legend: Readings on the Saints*, trans. William Granger Ryan (Princeton 1993), ii:82.
27 Gibson, *Theater of Devotion*, 167.
28 Among others, the possibilities suggested were that the speech provided a cover for the setting up of the pageant wagon; that it was a visible way to convey Thomas from one station to another; and that it was not meant to be spoken in its entirety but resembled a piano vamp, able to be exited whenever the rest of the cast was ready to begin.
29 Augustine, *Sermo 116*, vi.6, *PL* XXXVIII:659; *An Augustine Synthesis*, ed. and trans. Erich Przywara (London 1939), 223.
30 Warner, *Alone of All Her Sex*, 105–6.
31 Augustine, *Sermo 116*, vi.6, *PL* XXXVIII:659; Przywara, *Augustine Synthesis*, 223.
32 Augustine, *Sermo 192*, ii.2, *PL* XXXVIII:1011; Przywara, *Augustine Synthesis*, 244.
33 George A. Kennedy, *Classical Rhetoric and Its Christian and Secular Tradition from Ancient to Modern Times* (Chapel Hill 1980), 158.
34 Gibson, *Theater of Devotion*, 1–18.
35 Michael F.N. Dixon, *The Polliticke Courtier: Spenser's* The Faerie Queene *as a Rhetoric of Justice* (Montreal 1996), 32.

3. Mary Magdalene and Ethical Decorum

1 Helen Meredith Garth, *Saint Mary Magdalene in Mediaeval Literature* (Baltimore 1950), 98. Garth's own italics.
2 Robert H. Bowers, 'The Tavern Scene in the Middle English Digby Play of Mary Magdalene,' in *All These to Teach: Essays in Honor of C. A. Robertson*, ed. Robert A. Bryan et al. (Gainesville, FL 1965), 15–32.
3 Augustine, *De doctrina Christiana* iv.xix.38, pp. 244–5.
4 *Rhetorica ad Herennium*, ed. and trans. Harry Caplan, LCL 403 (Cambridge 1954), 254–5.
5 See also Charles Sears Baldwin, *Medieval Rhetoric and Poetic* (Gloucester, MA 1959), 68.
6 Lanham, *Handlist of Rhetorical Terms*, 45–6.

7 Huizinga, *Autumn of the Middle Ages*, 128–9.
8 Compare Hauser (*Introduction to Rhetorical Theory*, 189): '[I]n accepting the playwright's terms, we actually create a world with its own matrix of thoughts, emotions, and values as a proper motivational basis for action.'
9 P.J.P. Goldberg, 'Women,' in *Fifteenth-Century Attitudes: Perceptions of Society in Late Medieval England*, ed. Rosemary Horrox (Cambridge 1994), 127.
10 All references to *Mary Magdalene* are from *The Late Medieval Religious Plays of Bodleian MSS. Digby 133 and e Museo 160*, ed. Donald C. Baker, John L. Murphy, and Louis B. Hall Jr., EETS os 283 (Oxford 1982).
11 Susan Haskins, *Mary Magdalen: Myth and Metaphor* (London 1994), 3.
12 As Jacques Rossiaud notes, the loss or lack of a father was often said, in the fifteenth century, to drive young women to immoral behaviour. *Medieval Prostitution*, trans. Lydia G. Cochrane (London 1988), 142.
13 See also Marjorie M. Malvern, *Venus in Sackcloth: The Magdalen's Origins and Metamorphoses* (Carbondale 1975), 116–17.
14 It is notable also that when Mary Magdalene is visited by the Good Angel and told to repent, 'she does not have to be coaxed. Her conversion is sudden.' Malvern, *Venus in Sackcloth*, 118.
15 John W. Velz, 'Sovereignty in the Digby *Mary Magdalene*.' *Comparative Drama* 2 (1968), 32–43.
16 Garth, *Saint Mary Magdalene*, 64. Rossiaud also notes that Mary Magdalene was not always thought of as a prostitute or courtesan at this time; in fact, her wealthy background was sometimes given as direct evidence that she was neither. Some French preachers described her as merely an uncontrolled young woman similar to some daughters of the fifteenth-century nobility, whose behaviour and manner of dress, it was said, was breaking down the visual distinction between courtesans and noble ladies (*Medieval Prostitution*, 140–2). The Digby playwright's heroine seems to have a great deal in common with such continental portrayals.
17 Aristotle, *Rhetoric* ii.1.
18 Augustine, *De doctrina Christiana* iv.xxvii.59–60, pp. 276–7.
19 Gregory the Great, *Pastoral Care* II:3, trans. Henry Davis, *Ancient Christian Writers* XI (Westminster 1950), 48.
20 Aquinas, *Summa theologica* 2a2ae.177.2, XLV, *Prophecy and Other Charisms*, ed. and trans. Roland Potter (New York 1970), 132–3.
21 Osbern Bokenham, *Legendys of Hooly Wummen*, ed. Mary S. Serjentson, EETS os 206 (London 1938).
22 See Haskins, *Mary Magdalen*, 153; also 2 Kings (2 Sam.) 11 and Daniel 13.
23 Jacobus, *Legenda Aurea* I:629; *Golden Legend* I:375.
24 Jacobus, *Legenda Aurea* I:631; *Golden Legend* I:376–7.

25 *De doctrina Christiana* iv.xii.27, pp. 228–9.

26 Ibid., iv.xiii.29, pp. 232–3.

27 Augustine, 'Sermone Domini in Monte,' *Opera omnia*, XIV, ed. D.A.B. Caillau and D.M.N.S. Guillon (Paris 1838) I, XII, 33, p. 162; 'Our Lord's Sermon on the Mount,' *Works* VIII, ed. Marcus Dods (Edinburgh 1872), 26.

28 *De doctrina Christiana* iv.xvii.34, pp. 238–9.

29 'Sermone Domini in Monte' I, XII, 34, p. 163, 'Our Lord's Sermon on the Mount,' 27.

30 *De doctrina Christiana* iv.xii.27, pp. 228–9.

31 'Sermone Domine in Monte' I, XII, 34, p. 163, 'Our Lord's Sermon on the Mount,' 27.

32 *De doctrina Christiana* iv.xii.27, pp. 228–9.

33 'Sermone Domine in Monte' I, XII, 34, p. 163, 'Our Lord's Sermon on the Mount,' 27.

34 *De doctrina Christiana* iv.xii.27, pp. 230–1.

35 Ibid., iii.x.14–15, pp. 144–9. See also D.W. Robertson, Jr, *A Preface to Chaucer: Studies in Medieval Perspectives* (Princeton 1962), 295, for a classic, though now somewhat old-fashioned, perspective on the problem.

36 Velz, 'Sovereignty in the Digby *Mary Magdalene*,' 36.

37 Darryll Grantley, 'The Source of the Digby *Mary Magdalene*,' *Notes and Queries* 229 (1984), 457–9.

38 Jacobus, *Legenda Aurea*, I:631; *Golden Legend* I:376.

39 Augustine, *De doctrina Christiana* iv.xxv.55, pp. 272–3.

40 As the *Tretise of Miraclis Pleyinge* (102–3) declares, conversion is essentially the despising of empty signifiers.

41 Theresa Coletti, 'The Design of the Digby Play of *Mary Magdalene*,' *Studies in Philology* 76, no. 4 (1979), 330.

42 Jacobus, *Legenda aurea* I:628; *Golden Legend* I:375.

43 Jacobus, *Legenda aurea* I:628; *Golden Legend* I:374.

44 Kennedy, *Classical Rhetoric and Its Christian and Secular Tradition*, 157.

45 See William James, *The Varieties of Religious Experience: A Study in Human Nature*, 1902 (New York n.d.), 372.

46 'Stations of the Cross,' *The Oxford Dictionary of the Christian Church*, 3rd ed., ed. F.L. Cross and E.A. Livingstone (Oxford 1997), 1538–9.

47 See, for instance, *ad Herennium* iii.iv.26–iii.xxi.34, pp. 208–19; also Mary Carruthers, *The Book of Memory: A Study of Memory in Medieval Culture* (Cambridge 1990), 71–9. Although Carruthers notes that 'the architectural mnemonic,' as she calls it, was not the only such method (80), it seems to have been common in the rhetoric of pilgrimage and of devotion: witness the experiences of Margery Kempe at Jerusalem (*Book of Margery Kempe*,

66–75), in which devotion to particular places led to nostalgic experience of the most powerful kind. Margery Kempe was not alone in her manner of devotion; such devotion to holy places, and indeed to simulacra of holy places, had been common in the Mediterranean since antiquity, and with the Franciscan takeover of the shrines of the Holy Land in 1342, such devotion spread throughout Europe, eventually taking form in the devotion of the Stations of the Cross. See 'Stations of the Cross,' *The Harper Collins Encyclopedia of Catholicism*, gen. ed. Richard P. McBrien (San Francisco 1995), 1222. See Frances A. Yates, *The Art of Memory* (Chicago 1966), 50–128, for the most comprehensive treatment of architectural memory techniques.

48 In the *Legenda aurea*, this fact is even more explicit; the Queen tells her husband directly, 'sicut beatus Petrus te Iherosolimam duxit [...] sic et ego una cum beata Maria Magdalena duce et comite uobiscum fui et singula loca conspexi et conspecta memorie commendaui' (As blessed Peter conducted you to Jerusalem [...] I, with blessed Mary Magdalene as my guide and companion, was with you and committed all you saw to memory). Jacobus, *Legenda aurea* I:636; *Golden Legend* I:379.

49 Jacobus, *Legenda aurea* I:636; *Golden Legend* I:380.

50 Clifford Davidson, 'The Middle English Saint Play and Its Iconography,' in *The Saint Play in Medieval Europe*, ed. Clifford Davidson, EDAM 8 (Kalamazoo 1986), 93. The reference is to Bodleian MS Laud Lat. 15, fol. 20v.

51 Coletti ('Design,' 331) suggests that Mary Magdalene would appear 'in a hermit's garb' in the final scenes of this play, but there really is no indication of what exactly she is to wear, despite the 'rather conclusive evidence for the Digby playwright's attention to clothing in this part of the play.'

52 For the importance of food imagery in the play, see Coletti, 'Design' pp 316–25.

53 Davidson, 'Middle English Saint Play,' 71, 97.

54 Leon Eugene Lewis, 'The Play of *Mary Magdalene*,' *DAI* 23 (1963), 4685–6.

55 Hauser, *Introduction to Rhetorical Theory*, 100.

4. Joseph, Pathos, and the Audience

1 Francis L. Filas, in *Joseph, the Man Closest to Jesus: The Complete Life, Theology, and Devotional History of St. Joseph* (Boston 1962), 25–36, lists six apocryphal sources dealing with Joseph; of these, only the three discussed in the main text could have had any probable, direct effect upon the cycle plays because of content and chronology. The apocryphal sources cited are printed in English in several sources, including *The Apocryphal Gospels and Other Docu-*

ments Relating to the History of Christ, ed. B. Harris Cowper (London 1867), *The Lost Books of the Bible and the Forgotten Books of Eden* (Cleveland 1963), and *The Other Bible: Jewish Pseudographia, Christian Apocrypha, Gnostic Scriptures, Kabbalah, Dead Sea Scrolls*, ed. Willis Barnstone (San Francisco 1984), and are annotated extensively in E. Hennecke, *New Testament Apocrypha*, ed. W. Schneemelcher, trans. R. McL. Wilson, 2 vols (London 1963).

2 Warner, *Alone of All Her Sex*, 156.
3 Hennecke, *New Testament Apocrypha*, 406.
4 Cowper, *Apocryphal Gospels*, 14–15.
5 Ibid., 46.
6 Ibid., 46.
7 Filas, *Joseph*, 35.
8 Kolve, *Play Called Corpus Christi*, 249.
9 Bernard of Clairvaux, *Oeuvres Complètes*, ed. Marie-Imelda Huille and Joël Regnard (Paris 1993), 164–6. Henri Rondet, *Saint Joseph*, ed. and trans. Donald Attwater (New York 1956), 61–2.
10 Jean Gerson, *Oeuvres Complètes*, ed. Mgr Glorieux (Paris 1963), V:358. Rondet, *Saint Joseph*, 68.
11 Bernardine of Siena, 'Sermo II, De sancto Ioseph sponso beatae Virginis,' *Opera Omnia*, ed. Augustini Sepinski (Florence 1959), VII:358. *Saint Bernardine's Sermon on Saint Joseph*, trans. Eric May (Paterson, NJ 1947), 36.
12 Gerald T. Mahon, 'The Origin and Development of Devotion to Saint Joseph in England,' *Le Patronage de Saint Joseph: Actes du Congrès d'Études* (Montreal 1956), 175–92.
13 Éphrem Longpré, 'Saint Joseph et l'École Franciscaine du XIIIe siècle,' in *Le Patronage de Saint Joseph*, 237–46; Isa Ragusa and Rosalie B. Green, 'Introduction,' in *Meditations on the Life of Christ: An Illustrated Manuscript of the Fourteenth Century*, trans. Isa Ragusa, ed. Isa Ragusa and Rosalie B. Green (Princeton 1961), xxii, xxvi–xxvii.
14 Love, *Mirror*, 47.
15 Ibid., 52.
16 Ibid., 52.
17 Geoffrey of Vinsauf, *Poetria nova*, line 87. *The* Poetria nova *and Its Sources in Early Rhetorical Doctrine*, ed. Ernest Gallo (The Hague 1971), 18–19; *Poetria nova of Geoffrey of Vinsauf*, trans. Margaret F. Nims (Toronto 1967), 21–3.
18 Specht, 'Ethopoeia,' 5.
19 My observations and speculations concerning the play of 'Joseph's Trouble About Mary' are drawn largely from a production of the play that I directed, and that was performed in Toronto in the summer of 1995.

20 *ad Herennium*, 45.
21 Ibid., 18–19.
22 *Non-Cycle Plays and Fragments*, ed. Norman Davis, EETS ss 1 (London 1970), 43–57.
23 *ad Herennium*, 400–1.
24 'The Comic in the Cycles,' in *Medieval Drama*, ed. Neville Denny. Stratford-upon-Avon Studies 16 (London 1973), 114–15.
25 Hans Robert Jauss, *Aesthetic Experience and Literary Hermeneutics*, trans. Michael Shaw, Theory and History of Literature 3 (Minneapolis 1982), 191.
26 Epp, 'Visible Words,' 294.
27 Kenneth Burke, *A Rhetoric of Motives* (Berkeley 1962), 55–8.
28 Woolf, *English Mystery Plays*, 173.
29 Kolve, *Play Called Corpus Christi*, 247–8.
30 Mahon, 'Origin and Development,' 186–7.
31 Gibson, *Theater of Devotion*, 166.
32 Duffy, *Stripping of the Altars*, 102.
33 Kolve, *Play Called Corpus Christi*, 247–53.
34 *Towneley Plays* I:126–7.
35 Alexandra F. Johnston, 'The Word Made Flesh: Augustinian Elements in the York Cycle,' in *The Centre and Its Compass: Studies in Medieval Literature in Honor of Professor John Leyerle*, ed. Robert A. Taylor et al. (Kalamazoo 1993), 225–46.
36 *In Joannis Evangelium tractatus* xxix.6, *PL* XXXV:1630. My translation.
37 '[V]ides aliquid, ut credas aliquid, et ex eo quod vides, credas quod non vides' (You see something so that you may believe something, and from what you do see you may believe what you don't see), *Sermo* 126, ii.3, *PL* XXXVIII:699; and 'Dupliciter ducimur, auctoritate atque ratione' (We are led in two ways, by authority and by reason), *De ordine libri ii* 2, ix.26, *PL* XXXII:1007. My translations.
38 *ad Herennium*, 198–9.
39 Beadle, *York Plays*, 437; *The York Play: A Facsimile of British Library MS Additional 35290, Together with a Facsimile of the Ordo Paginarum Section of the A/Y Memorandum Book*, ed. Richard Beadle and Peter Meredith (Leeds 1983), f 75.
40 Warner, *Alone of All Her Sex*, 189.
41 Love, *Mirror*, 51.
42 *REED: York*, ed. Johnston and Rogerson, 19, 351, 705.
43 *The First and Second Prayer Books of Edward VI*, ed. E.C.S. Gibson (London 1960), 278, 428.

44 David Cressy, *Birth, Marriage, and Death: Ritual, Religion, and the Life-Cycle in Tudor and Stuart England* (Oxford 1997), 208.

45 Cressy, *Birth, Marriage, and Death*, 210.

46 Keith Thomas, *Religion and the Decline of Magic: Studies in Popular Beliefs in Sixteenth- and Seventeenth-Century England* (1971, repr. London 1991), 43; see Cressy 208ff.

47 *REED: York*, ed. Johnston and Rogerson, 351.

48 Cressy, *Birth, Marriage, and Death*, 228–9.

49 Warner, *Alone of All Her Sex*, 188–90.

50 'Et erat pater eius et mater mirantes super his quae dicebantur de illo' (And his father and mother were wondering at those things which were spoken concerning him [Luke 2:33]).

5. Paul and the Rhetoric of Sainthood

1 An area that has been explored by Mary del Villar, 'The Staging of *The Conversion of Saint Paul*,' *Theatre Notebook* 25 (1970–1), 64–8; Glynne Wickham, 'The Staging of Saint Plays in England,' in *The Medieval Drama*, ed. Sandro Sticca (Albany 1972), 99–119; Darryll Grantley, 'Saints' Plays,' in *The Cambridge Companion to Medieval English Theatre*, ed. Richard Beadle (Cambridge 1994), 265–89; and Raymond J. Pentzell, 'The Medieval Theatre in the Streets,' *Theatre Survey* 14 (1973), 1–21. On the question of whether or not the audience moved in procession with the play, my own opinion is that they did, and I shall treat the play accordingly. This opinion is based upon my experience as producer of just such a production, done by Poculi Ludique Societas in 1994. See also John Marshall, 'Modern Productions of Medieval English Plays,' in *Cambridge Companion*, ed. Beadle, 305–6.

2 Baker, Murphy, and Hall, *Late Medieval Religious Plays*, xviii. See also Donald C. Baker, 'When Is a Text a Play? Reflections Upon What Certain Late Medieval Dramatic Texts Can Tell Us,' in *Contexts for Early English Drama*, ed. Marianne G. Briscoe and John C. Coldewey (Bloomington 1989), 20–5.

3 Janette Dillon, *Language and Stage in Medieval and Renaissance England* (Cambridge 1998), 76.

4 Hill-Vasquez, 'Possibilities of Performance,' 3.

5 Quoted in *Late Medieval Religious Plays*, 195, nn. 11–12. My translation.

6 See Kennedy, *Classical Rhetoric and Its Christian and Secular Tradition*, 130, for a summary of rhetorical scholarship on Paul's epistles themselves.

7 Augustine, *De doctrina Christiana*, iv.xv.46, p. 214. Green paraphrases 'eloquentem nostrum' as 'the paragon of Christian eloquence,' 215.

8 Murphy, *Rhetoric in the Middle Ages*, 282.

9 Augustine, *De doctrina Christiana*, x.xxiv.66, pp. 224–5.

10 Thomas Aquinas, *Summa theologica*, XLV, 2a2ae, 177,1, *Prophecy and Other Charisms*, 130–1. Note, however, Aquinas's emphasis on the role of the audience in completing the orator's speech.

11 Baker, Murphy, and Hall, *Late Medieval Religious Plays*, xxiv.

12 Jacobus, *Legenda aurea* I:199; *Golden Legend* I:120.

13 My thanks to Kimberley M. Yates for pointing this out to me.

14 David Mills, '"Look at Me When I'm Speaking to You": The "Behold and See" Convention in Medieval Drama,' *METh* 7 (1985), 4–12.

15 Baker, Murphy, and Hall, *Late Medieval Religious Plays*, xxv.

16 Geoffrey Chaucer, *The Parson's Tale* X.420. *The Riverside Chaucer*, gen. ed. Larry D. Benson (Boston 1987).

17 John Coldewey, 'The Digby Plays and the Chelmsford Records,' *RORD* 18 (1975), 103–21.

18 Karl Young, *The Drama of the Medieval Church* (Oxford 1933), II:222.

19 My thanks to Clifford Davidson for pointing this out to me.

20 Luba Eleen, 'The Illumination of the Pauline Epistles in French and English Bibles of the Twelfth and Thirteenth Centuries,' PhD diss., University of Toronto 1972, I:193–6. Eleen catalogues these and several other western conventions of portraying Paul's journey.

21 Jacobus, *Legenda aurea* I:198; *Golden Legend* I:119.

22 Jacobus, *Legenda aurea* I:200; *Golden Legend* I:120.

23 Jacobus, *Legenda aurea* I:199; *Golden Legend* I:119. These seem to be Jacobus's own words, not Augustine's.

24 Victor I. Scherb, 'Frame Structure in *The Conversion of St. Paul*,' *Comparative Drama* 26 (1992), 127.

25 Young, *Drama of the Medieval Church*, II:220.

26 See, for instance, Love, *Mirror*, 176–7, in which the reader is told, 'Now take hede diligently to þe manner of crucifying,' and is then told in great detail how it was done, only to be informed, 'Þis is one maner of his crucifying after þe opinione of sume men. Oþere þere bene þat trowen þat he was not crucifiede in þis manere'; the reader is then shown an entirely different method in equal detail. The point, however, is not to teach history but to move the reader emotionally and spiritually: 'Bot wheþer so it be in one maner or in oþere soþe it is þat oure lorde Jesus was nailede hard vpon þe crosse.' Some versions of the *Meditationes* add that the reader may choose one version or the other to contemplate 'If this suits you better.' *Meditations on the Life of Christ*, ed. Ragusa and Green, 334.

27 del Villar, 'The Staging of *The Conversion of Saint Paul*,' 66.

28 Cited in the *OED*'s entry under 'affection,' def. 3. The *MED*'s entry under 'affeccioun' similarly defines the word as the 'faculty of the soul concerned with emotion and volition.'

29 Chaucer, *The Parson's Tale* X.728.

30 Performance experience shows different possibilities in different audiences. During one of PLS's performances in 1994, to an audience of high school students in Hamilton NY, the audience crowded so thickly around Saul that he was scarcely able to make his own progress, leading the actor to snap, 'Out of the way, peasants!' By contrast, a mostly adult audience in Toronto a week later kept its distance, prompting the actor to encourage them to follow when they would not.

31 *Book of Margery Kempe*, 86.

32 Some versions of the Vulgate have at Acts 9:5, 'durum est tibi contra stimulum calcitrare' (It is hard for thee to kick against the goad); this phrase also appears at Acts 26:14 in all versions. Although no Greek manuscript has the phrase at 9:5, the influence of the Vulgate was still such during the sixteenth century, the period of this play's provenance, that Erasmus's 1516 Greek New Testament transposes the phrase to 9:5, following the Vulgate's example. See Bruce M. Metzger, *A Textual Commentary on the Greek New Testament*, 2nd ed (New York 1994), 318. The phrase originates in Euripedes' *Bacchae*, at lines 794–5. Jeff S. Dailey's attribution of the phrase's origins to Wyclif is incorrect: 'Saint Paul's Horse and Related Problems,' *RORD* 41 (2002), 199–202.

33 Robert of Basevorn, *The Form of Preaching (Forma praedicandi)*, trans. Leopold Krul, *Three Medieval Rhetorical Arts*, ed. James J. Murphy (Berkeley 1971), 129.

34 Baker, Murphy, and Hall, *Late Medieval Religious Plays*, 196, n. 502.

35 Duffy, *Stripping of the Altars*, 220.

36 See also Dillon, *Language and Stage*, 70–105, on the politics of multilingual plays in Tudor England.

37 At line 29: 'O ʒe souerens þat sytt and ʒe brothern þat stonde ryght wppe.' *The Macro Plays*, ed. Mark Eccles, EETS os 262 (London 1969), 155.

38 In this way the Digby play differs significantly from French and Latin plays on the same subject. Scherb, 'Frame Structure,' 130.

39 In PLS's 1992 production, directed by Kimberley M. Yates, Saul tore his proud knightly clothes off at this moment to reveal something like a penitent's shift beneath; it was a neatly made connection between the two sins.

40 Jadwiga S. Smith, 'The English Medieval Conversion Plays and the Doctrine of St. Augustine,' *Medieval Perspectives* 3 (1988), 246.

41 The line is sometimes quoted as 'both man and best,' which is indeed what

appears in Baker, Murphy, and Hall's edition, 18, line 515. However, that line was written by the scribe who inserted the devils' scene, and is recopied at that point in the manuscript, probably to allow ease of reading. The original text, which is crossed out before the interpolation of the devils, reads 'most and lest,' and appears in Baker, Murphy, and Hall, 15. The earlier reading, it seems to me, makes more sense in context. Both Furnivall and Bevington prefer the 'most and lest' reading in their editions, though Coldewey prefers 'man and best.' See *The Digby Plays*, ed. F.J. Furnivall, EETS es 70 (London 1896), 47; *Medieval Drama*, ed. David Bevington (Boston 1975), 682, and *Early English Drama: An Anthology*, ed. John C. Coldewey (New York 1993), 181.

42 Dillon, *Language and Stage*, 31–50.
43 I use the term 'opacity' descriptively, not pejoratively, following Richard Lanham, *The Motives of Eloquence: Literary Rhetoric in the Renaissance* (New Haven 1976), 26.
44 Dillon, *Language and Stage*, 51.
45 John W. Velz, 'From Jerusalem to Damascus: Bilocal Dramaturgy in Medieval and Shakespearean Conversion Plays,' *Comparative Drama* 15 (1981–2), 313: 'The conversion is unanticipated, without gradation, entire.'
46 Compare, for instance, the king of Marseilles's appeals to the idol in the play of *Mary Magdalene*, lines 1538–77.
47 Johnston, 'Word Made Flesh,' 235.
48 Hill-Vasquez, 'Possibilities of Performance,' 5.
49 Ibid., 18, n. 29.
50 Ibid., 6.
51 On the contrary, in my own experience it is this scene which makes the evil of Annas, Caiaphas, and the pre-conversion Saul completely unambiguous; though our audiences enjoyed laughing at the devils, nobody followed them or seemed to want their attention.
52 Duffy, *Stripping of the Altars*, 180.
53 Peter Happé, 'The Protestant Adaptation of the Saint Play,' *The Saint Play in Medieval Europe*, 214.

6. Conclusion

1 T.S. Eliot, 'Journey of the Magi,' in *The Complete Poems and Plays: 1909–1950* (New York 1962), 68–9. Line numbers are cited in the text.
2 T.S. Eliot, 'A Song for Simeon,' in *Complete Poems and Plays*, 69–70.
3 Stanley Fish, *Surprised by Sin: The Reader in* Paradise Lost, 2nd ed. (Cambridge, MA 1997), 6.

4 Augustine, despite his arguments for the necessity of God's grace, nonetheless insists that humanity's acceptance of that grace is voluntary, not forced See, for instance, *De spiritu et littera*, ed. William Bright (Oxford 1914) 21.54, 34.60.
5 Fish, *Surprised by Sin*, 6.
6 Augustine, *De doctrina Christiana* iv.i.4, pp. 196–7.
7 Ibid., iv.ii. 4–5, pp. 196–9.
8 Duffy, *Stripping of the Altars*, 68.
9 W.H. Auden, 'For the Time Being,' in *Collected Poems*, ed. Edward Mendelson (New York 1991), 365.

Bibliography

Antin, David. 'Modernism and Postmodernism: Approaching the Present in American Poetry.' *Boundary* 2.1 (Fall 1972): 98–133.

Aquinas, Thomas. *Expositiones in Job. Opera omnia.* Vol. 18. Ed. S.E. Fretté. Paris, 1976.

– *Summa theologica.* Vol. 45, *Prophecy and Other Charisms.* Ed. and trans. Roland Potter. New York, 1970.

– *The Sunday Sermons of the Great Fathers* [*Catena Aurea*]. Ed. and trans. M.F. Toal. 4 vols. Chicago, 1958.

Aristotle. *Rhetoric.* Trans. W. Rhys Roberts. *The Works of Aristotle.* Vol. 1. Ed. W.D. Ross. Oxford: Oxford UP, n.d.; repr. Chicago, 1952.

Atkinson, Clarissa W. *Mystic and Pilgrim: The Book and the World of Margery Kempe.* Ithaca, 1983.

Auden, W.H. 'For the Time Being.' In *Collected Poems.* Ed. Edward Mendelson, 347–400. New York, 1991.

Augustine. *An Augustine Synthesis.* Ed. and trans. Erich Przywara. London, 1939.

– *Confessions.* Trans. Henry Chadwick. Oxford, 1992.

– *De doctrina Christiana.* Ed. and trans. R.P.H. Green. Oxford, 1995.

– *De spiritu et littera.* Ed. William Bright. Oxford, 1914.

– *The Essential Augustine.* Ed. Vernon J. Bourke. Indianapolis, 1974.

– 'In Joannis Evangelium tractatus 121.' *Opera Omnia.* Vol. 16. Ed. D.A.B. Caillau. Paris, 1838.

– *On Christian Teaching.* Trans. R.P.H. Green. Oxford, 1997.

– 'De ordine libri II.' *Patrologia Latina.* Ed. J.-P. Migne. Vol. 32. Paris, 1902.

– 'Our Lord's Sermon on the Mount.' *Works.* Ed. Marcus Dods. Vol. 8. Edinburgh, 1872.

– 'Sermo 116.' *Patrologia Latina.* Ed. J.-P. Migne. Vol. 38. Paris, 1865.

- 'Sermo 192.' *Patrologia Latina*. Ed. J.-P. Migne. Vol. 38. Paris, 1865.
- 'Sermone Domini in Monte.' *Opera Omnia*. Ed. D.A.B. Caillau and D.M.N.S. Guillon. Vol. 14. Paris, 1838.

Baird, Joseph L., and Lorrayne Y. Baird. 'Fabliau Form and the Hegge *Joseph's Return*.' *Chaucer Review* 8.2 (1973): 159–69.

Baker, Donald C. 'When Is a Play a Text? Reflections Upon What Certain Late Medieval Dramatic Texts Can Tell Us.' In *Contexts for Early English Drama*. Ed. Briscoe and Coldewey, 20–40.

Baldwin, Charles Sears. *Mediaeval Rhetoric and Poetic*. Gloucester, MA, 1959.

Barnstone, Willis, ed. *The Other Bible: Jewish Pseudographia, Christian Apocrypha, Gnostic Scriptures, Kabbalah, Dead Sea Scrolls*. San Francisco, 1984.

Beadle, Richard, ed. *The Cambridge Companion to Medieval English Theatre*. Cambridge, 1994.

Bernard of Clairvaux. *Oeuvres Complètes*. Ed. Marie-Imelda Huille and Joël Regnard. Paris, 1993.

Bernardine of Siena. *Opera omnia*. Ed. Augustini Sepinski. Vol. 7. Florence, 1959.

- *Saint Bernardine's Sermon on Saint Joseph*. Trans. Eric May. Paterson, NJ, 1947.

Bevington, David, ed. *Medieval Drama*. Boston, 1975.

Biblia Sacra iuxta vulgatam versionem. 4th ed. Ed. B. Fischer et al. Stuttgart, 1994.

Bitzer, Lloyd. 'The Rhetorical Situation.' *Philosophy and Rhetoric* 1 (1968): 1–15.

Bokenham, Osbern. *Legendys of Hooly Wummen*. Ed. Mary S. Serjentson. EETS os 206. London, 1938.

Booth, Wayne C. *The Rhetoric of Fiction*. 2nd ed. Chicago, 1983.

Bowers, Robert H. 'The Tavern Scene in the Middle English Digby Play of Mary Magdalene.' In *All These to Teach: Essays in Honor of C. A. Robertson*. Ed. Robert A. Bryan et al., 15–32. Gainesville, 1965.

Brawer, Robert A. 'The Characterization of Pilate in the York Cycle Play.' *Studies in Philology* 69 (1972): 289–303.

Brecht, Bertolt. *Brecht on Theatre*. Ed. and trans. John Willett. New York, 1964.

Briscoe, Marianne G., and John C. Coldewey, eds. *Contexts for Early English Drama*. Bloomington, 1989.

Brown, Peter. *The Cult of the Saints: Its Rise and Function within Latin Antiquity*. Chicago, 1981.

Buchheimer, Arnold. 'The Development of Ideas About Empathy.' *Journal of Counseling Psychology* 10.1 (1963): 61–70.

Burke, Kenneth. *A Rhetoric of Motives*. Berkeley, 1962.

Bynum, Caroline Walker. *The Resurrection of the Body in Western Christianity, 200–1336*. New York, 1995.

Caplan, Harry. *Of Eloquence: Studies in Ancient and Medieval Rhetoric*. Ed. Anne King and Helen North. Ithaca, 1970.

Carpenter, Sarah. 'Morality-Play Characters.' *Medieval English Theatre* 5 (1983): 18–28.

Carruthers, Mary. *The Book of Memory: A Study of Memory in Medieval Culture*. Cambridge Studies in Medieval Literature 10. Cambridge, 1990.

Chambers, E.K. *The Mediaeval Stage*. 2 vols. Oxford, 1903. Repr. 1 vol. Mineola, NY, 1996.

Chaucer, Geoffrey. *The Riverside Chaucer*. Ed. Larry D. Benson. Boston, 1987.

The Chester Mystery Cycle. Ed. R.M. Lumiansky and David Mills. EETS ss 3, 9. London, 1974, 1986.

Chrysostom. 'Homilia 87 in Joannis evangelium.' *Collectio selecta SS. ecclesiae patrum*. Ed. D.A.B. Caillau and D.M.N.S. Guillon. Vol. 79. Paris, 1835.

Cicero. *De inventione, De optimo genere oratorum, Topica*. Ed. and trans. H.M. Hubbell. Loeb Classical Library 386. Cambridge, MA, 1949.

Clopper, Lawrence M. '*Communitas*: The Play of Saints in Late Medieval England.' *Mediaevalia* 18 (1995): 81–110.

– '*Miracula* and *The Tretise of Miraclis Pleyinge*.' *Speculum* 65 (1990): 878–905.

– 'Tyrants and Villains: Characterization in the Passion Sequences of the English Cycle Plays.' *Modern Language Quarterly* 41 (1980): 3–20.

Clopper, Lawrence M., ed. *Records of Early English Drama: Chester*. Toronto, 1979.

Coldewey, John C. 'The Digby Plays and the Chelmsford Records.' *Research Opportunities in Renaissance Drama* 18 (1975): 103–21.

– 'The Non-Cycle Plays and the East Anglian Tradition.' In *Cambridge Companion*. Ed. Beadle, 189–210.

Coldewey, John C., ed. *Early English Drama: An Anthology*. New York, 1993.

Coletti, Theresa. 'The Design of the Digby Plays of *Mary Magdalene*.' *Studies in Philology* 76:4 (1979): 313–33.

Conley, Thomas M. *Rhetoric in the European Tradition*. Chicago, 1990.

The Cornish Ordinalia: A Medieval Dramatic Trilogy. Trans. Markham Harris. Washington, DC, 1969.

Cowper, B. Harris, ed. *The Apocryphal Gospels and Other Documents Relating to the History of Christ*. London, 1867.

Cressy, David. *Birth, Marriage, and Death: Ritual, Religion, and the Life-Cycle in Tudor and Stuart England*. Oxford, 1997.

Cross, F.L., and E.A. Livingstone, eds. *The Oxford Dictionary of the Christian Church*. 3rd ed. Oxford, 1997.

Curtius, E.R. *European Literature and the Latin Middle Ages*. Trans. Willard R. Trask. Bollingen Series 34. Princeton, 1953.

Cushman, Lysander W. *The Devil and the Vice in English Dramatic Literature Before Shakespeare*. Halle, 1900.

Dailey, Jeff S. 'Saint Paul's Horse and Related Problems.' *Research Opportunities in Renaissance Drama* 41 (2002): 199–202.

Davidson, Clifford. 'The Digby *Mary Magdalene* and the Magdalene Cult of the Middle Ages.' *Annuale Mediaevale* 13 (1972): 70–87.

– 'The Middle English Saint Play and Its Iconography.' In *Saint Play*. Ed. Davidson, 31–122.

– 'Northern Spirituality and the Late Medieval Drama of York.' In *The Spirituality of Western Christendom*. Ed. E.R. Elder, 125–208. Kalamazoo, 1976.

– 'Saints in Play: English Theater and Saints' Lives.' In *Saints*. Ed. Sticca, 145–60.

Davidson, Clifford, ed. *The Saint Play in Medieval Europe*. Early Drama, Art, and Music Monograph Series 8. Kalamazoo, 1986.

Davies, Robertson. 'Making the Best of Second Best.' In *A Voice from the Attic: Essays on the Art of Reading*, 147–89. Rev. ed. New York, 1990.

Davis, Mark H. *Empathy: A Social Psychological Approach*. Madison, WI, 1994.

Deasy, C. Philip. *St. Joseph in the English Mystery Plays*. Washington, 1937.

del Villar, Mary. 'The Staging of *The Conversion of Saint Paul*.' *Theatre Notebook* 25 (1970–1): 64–8.

Denny, Neville, ed. *Medieval Drama*. London, 1973.

Digby Plays. See *Late Medieval Religious Plays*.

The Digby Plays: Facsimiles of the Plays in Bodley MSS Digby 133 and E Museo 160. Ed. Donald C. Baker and James L. Murphy. Leeds, 1976.

The Digby Plays with an Incomplete 'Morality' of Wisdom, Who Is Christ, ed. F.J. Furnivall. EETS es. 70. London, 1896.

Dillon, Janette. *Language and Stage in Medieval and Renaissance England*. Cambridge, 1998.

Dives and Pauper. Ed. Priscilla Heath Barnum. EETS os 275. Oxford, 1976.

Dixon, Michael F.N. *The Polliticke Courtier: Spenser's* The Faerie Queene *as a Rhetoric of Justice*. Montreal, 1996.

Duffy, Eamon. *The Stripping of the Altars: Traditional Religion in England 1400–1580*. New Haven, 1992.

Dunn, E. Catherine. 'The Literary Style of the Towneley Plays.' *American Benedictine Review* 20 (1969): 481–504.

– 'Popular Devotion in the Vernacular Drama of Medieval England.' *Medievalia et Humanistica* 4 (1973): 55–68.

Eleen, Luba. 'The Illumination of the Pauline Epistles in French and English Bibles of the Twelfth and Thirteenth Centuries.' 2 vols. Diss. U of Toronto, 1972.

Eliot, T.S. *The Complete Poems and Plays: 1909–1950*. New York, 1962.

– 'Journey of the Magi.' *Complete Poems*, 68–9.

– 'A Song for Simeon.' *Complete Poems*, 69–70.

Elliott, John R. 'Medieval Acting.' In *Contexts for Early English Drama*. Ed. Briscoe and Coldewey, 238–51.

Enders, Jody. *The Medieval Theater of Cruelty: Rhetoric, Memory, Violence*. Ithaca, NY, 1999.

Enders, Jody. *Rhetoric and the Origins of Medieval Drama*. Ithaca, NY, 1992.

Epp, Garrett P.J. 'Visible Words: The York Plays, Brecht, and Gestic Writing.' *Comparative Drama* 24 (1990–1): 289–305.

Ferster, Judith. 'Writing on the Ground: Interpretation in Chester Play XII.' *Sign, Sentence, Discourse: Language in Medieval Thought and Literature*. Syracuse, 1989. 179–93.

Filas, Francis L. *Joseph, the Man Closest to Jesus: The Complete Life, Theology, and Devotional History of St. Joseph*. Boston, 1962.

The First and Second Prayer Books of Edward VI. Ed. E.C.S. Gibson. London, 1960.

Fish, Stanley. *Is There a Text in This Class? The Authority of Interpretive Communities*. Cambridge, MA, 1980.

– *Self-Consuming Artifacts: The Experience of Seventeenth-Century Literature*. Berkeley, 1972.

– *Surprised by Sin: The Reader in* Paradise Lost. 2nd ed. Cambridge, MA, 1997.

Frye, Northrop. *Anatomy of Criticism: Four Essays*. Princeton, 1957.

Gardiner, Harold C. *Mysteries' End: An Investigation of the Last Days of the Medieval Religious Stage*. New Haven, 1946.

Garth, Helen Meredith. *Saint Mary Magdalene in Mediaeval Literature*. Baltimore, 1950.

Geoffrey of Vinsauf. *Poetria nova*. Trans. Margaret F. Nims. Mediaeval Sources in Translation 6. Toronto, 1967.

– *Poetria nova. The* Poetria nova *and Its Sources in Early Rhetorical Doctrine*. Ed. Ernest Gallo. The Hague, 1971.

– *The New Poetics*. Trans. Jane Baltzell Kopp. In *Three Medieval Rhetorical Arts*. Ed. Murphy, 27–108.

Gerson, Jean. *Oeuvres Complètes*, ed. Mgr Glorieux. Paris, 1963.

Gibson, Gail McMurray. 'The Images of Doubt and Belief: Visual Symbolism in the Middle English Plays of Joseph's Trouble about Mary.' Diss. U of Virginia, 1975.

– 'Porta Haec Clausa Erit: Comedy, Conception, and Ezekiel's Closed Door in the *Ludus Coventriae* Play of "Joseph's Return."' *Journal of Medieval and Renaissance Studies* 8 (1978): 137–57.

– *The Theater of Devotion: East Anglian Drama and Society in the Late Middle Ages.* Chicago, 1989.

Goldberg, P.J.P. 'Women.' In *Fifteenth-Century Attitudes.* Ed. Horrox, 112–31.

Grantley, Darryll. 'Saints' Plays.' In *Cambridge Companion.* Ed. Beadle, 265–89.

– 'The Source of the Digby *Mary Magdalene.*' *Notes and Queries* 229 (1984): 457–9.

Gregory the Great. 'Homily 26.' *XL Homilarum in evangelia.* Book 2. *Patrologia Latina.* Ed. J.-P. Migne. Vol. 76. Paris, 1849.

– *Moralia in Job. Patrologia Latina.* Ed. J.-P. Migne. Vol. 75. Paris, 1849.

– *Pastoral Care.* Trans. Henry Dans. Ancient Christian Writers XI. Westminster,, 1950.

Haman, Mark Stefan. 'The Introspective and Egocentric Quests of Character and Audience: Modes of Self-Definition in the York Corpus Christi Cycle and in Chaucer's "Merchant's Tale."' Diss. U of Rochester, 1982.

Happé, Peter. 'A Guide to Criticism of Medieval English Theatre.' In *Cambridge Companion.* Ed. Beadle, 312–43.

– 'The Protestant Adaptation of the Saint Play.' In *Saint Play.* Ed. Davidson, 205–40.

Happé, Peter, ed. *The Complete Plays of John Bale.* Vol. 1. Cambridge, 1985.

Hardison, O.B., Jr. *Christian Rite and Christian Drama in the Middle Ages: Essays in the Origin and Early History of Modern Drama.* Baltimore, 1965.

Haskins, Susan. *Mary Magdalen: Myth and Metaphor.* London, 1994.

Hauser, Arnold. *The Social History of Art.* Trans. Stanley Goodman. New York, 1952.

Hauser, Gerard A. *Introduction to Rhetorical Theory.* Prospect Heights, IL, 1986.

Hennecke, E. *New Testament Apocrypha.* Ed. W. Schneemelcher. Trans. R. McL. Wilson. 2 vols. London, 1963.

Hill-Vasquez, Heather. 'The Possibilities of Performance: A Reformation Sponsorship for the Digby *Conversion of Saint Paul.*' *REED Newsletter* 22.1 (1997): 2–20.

Holy Bible [Douay-Rheims version]. New York, 1941.

Holy Bible: Holy Trinity Edition [Confraternity Version], ed. John P. O'Connell. Chicago, 1951.

Horrox, Rosemary, ed. *Fifteenth-Century Attitudes: Perceptions of Society in Late Medieval England.* Cambridge, 1994.

Howard, Donald. *The Three Temptations: Medieval Man in Search of the World.* Princeton, 1996.

Huizinga, Johan. *The Autumn of the Middle Ages.* Trans. Rodney J. Payton and Ulrich Mammitzsch. Chicago, 1996. Trans. of *Herfsttij der Middeleeuwen*, 2nd ed., 1921.

Iser, Wolfgang. *The Act of Reading: A Theory of Aesthetic Response*. Baltimore, 1978.

Jacobus de Voragine. *The Golden Legend: Readings on the Saints*. Trans. William Granger Ryan. 2 vols. Princeton, 1993.

– [Iacopo da Varazze]. *Legenda Aurea*. Ed. Giovanni Paolo Maggioni. 2 vols. Sismel, 1998.

James, William. *The Varieties of Religious Experience: A Study in Human Nature*. 1902. New York, n.d.

Jauss, Hans Robert. *Aesthetic Experience and Literary Hermeneutics*. Trans. Michael Shaw. Theory and History of Literature 3. Minneapolis, 1982.

Jeffrey, David L. 'English Saints' Plays.' In *Medieval Drama*. Ed. Denny, 69–89.

Johnston, Alexandra F. 'Acting Mary: The Emotional Realism of the Mature Virgin in the N-Town Plays.' In *From Page to Performance: Essays in Early English Drama*. Ed. John Alford, 85–98. East Lansing, 1995.

– 'English Community Drama in Crisis, 1535–80.' In *European Communities of Medieval Drama: A Collection of Essays*. Ed. Alan Hindley, 248–69. Turnhout, 1999.

– 'Performance Practise Informed by Image: The Iconography of the Chester Pageants.' In *Spectacle and Image in Renaissance Europe: Selected Papers of the XXIInd Conference at the Centre d'Études Supérieurs de la Renaissance de Tours, 29 June-8 July 1989*. Ed. André Lascombes, 245–62. Lieden, 1993.

– 'The Word Made Flesh: Augustinian Elements in the York Cycle.' In *The Centre and Its Compass: Studies in Medieval Literature in Honor of Professor John Leyerle*. Ed. Robert A. Taylor et al., 225–46. Studies in Medieval Culture 3. Kalamazoo, 1993.

Johnston, Alexandra F., and Margaret Rogerson, eds. *Records of Early English Drama: York*. Toronto, 1979.

Julian of Norwich. *A Book of Showings to the Anchoress Julian of Norwich*. Ed. Edmund College and James Walsh. Toronto, 1978.

Kahrl, Stanley H. *Traditions of Medieval English Drama*. London, 1974.

Kempe, Margery. *The Book of Margery Kempe*. Ed. Sanford Brown Meech and Hope Emily Allen. EETS os 212. London, 1940.

Kennedy, George A. *Classical Rhetoric and Its Christian and Secular Tradition from Ancient to Modern Times*. Chapel Hill, 1980.

Kolve, V.A. *The Play Called Corpus Christi*. Princeton, NJ, 1966.

Langland, William. *The Vision of Piers Plowman: A Critical Edition of the B-Text Based on Trinity College Cambridge MS B. 15. 17*. Ed. A.V.C. Schmidt. 2nd ed. Everyman. London, 1995.

Lanham, Richard A. *A Handlist of Rhetorical Terms*. 2nd ed. Berkeley, 1991.

– *The Motives of Eloquence: Literary Rhetoric in the Renaissance*. New Haven, 1976.

The Late Medieval Religious Plays of Bodleian MSS. Digby 133 and e Museo 160. Ed. Donald C. Baker, John L. Murphy, and Louis B. Hall Jr. EETS os 283. Oxford, 1982.

LeVert, Laurelle Marie. 'The Rhetoric of Response: Affectivity and Didacticism in Middle English Devotional Experiences of the Passion.' Diss. U of Toronto, 1999.

Lewis, C.S. *The Discarded Image: An Introduction to Medieval and Renaissance Literature*. Cambridge, 1964.

Lewis, Leon Eugene. 'The Play of *Mary Magdalene*.' *Dissertation Abstracts International* 23 (1963): 4685–6.

Longpré, Éphrem, 'Saint Joseph et l'École Franciscaine de XIIIe Siécle,' *Le Patronage de Saint Joseph* 237–46.

Lost Books of the Bible and the Forgotten Books of Eden. Cleveland, 1963.

Love, Nicholas. *Nicholas Love's Mirror of the Blessed Life of Jesus Christ: A Critical Edition Based on Cambridge University Library Additional MSS 6578 and 6686*. Ed. Michael G. Sargent. Garland Medieval Texts 18. New York, 1992.

Lydgate, John. 'Ballade at the Reverence of Our Lady.' *Lydgate's Minor Poems*. Ed. H.N. MacCracken. Vol. 1. EETS es 107. Oxford, 1910.

The Macro Plays. Ed. Mark Eccles. EETS o.s. 262. London, 1969.

Mahon, Gerald T. 'The Origin and Development of Devotion to Saint Joseph in England.' In *Le Patronage de Saint Joseph* 175–92.

Maltman, Sister Nicholas. 'Light in and on the Digby *Mary Magdalene*.' In *Saints, Scholars, and Heroes: Studies in Medieval Culture in Honor of Charles W. Jones*. Ed. Margot H. King and Wesley M. Stevens, 257–80. Vol. 1. Collegeville, MN, 1979.

Malvern, Marjorie M. *Venus in Sackcloth: The Magdalen's Origins and Metamorphoses*. Carbondale, 1975.

Marshall, John. 'Modern Productions of Medieval English Plays.' In *Cambridge Companion*. Ed. Beadle, 290–311.

McBrien, Richard P., gen. ed. *The Harper Collins Encyclopedia of Catholicism*. San Francisco, 1995.

Meditations on the Life of Christ: An Illustrated Manuscript of the Fourteenth Century. Trans. Isa Ragusa. Ed. Isa Ragusa and Rosalie B. Green. Princeton, NJ, 1961.

Meredith, Peter. 'John Clerke's Hand in the York Register.' *Leeds Studies in English*. New Series 12 (1981): 245–71.

Meredith, Peter. 'The Towneley Cycle.' In *Cambridge Companion*. Ed. Beadle, 134–62.

Meredith, Peter, ed. *The Mary Play from the N.town Manuscript*. Rev. 2nd ed. Exeter, 1997.

– ed. *The Passion Play from the N.town Manuscript*. London, 1990.

Metzger, Bruce M. *A Textual Commentary on the Greek New Testament*. 2nd ed. New York, 1994.

Miller, Joseph M., Michael H. Prosser, and Thomas W. Benson, eds. *Readings in Medieval Rhetoric*. Bloomington, 1973.

Mills, David. 'Characterisation in the English Mystery Plays: A Critical Prologue.' *Medieval English Theatre* 5 (1983): 5–17.

– 'The Chester Cycle.' In *Cambridge Companion*. Ed. Beadle, 109–33.

– '"Look at Me When I'm Speaking to You": The "Behold and See" Convention in Medieval Drama.' *Medieval English Theatre* 7 (1985): 4–12.

– 'Religious Drama and Civic Ceremonial.' *The* Revels *History of Drama in English*. Vol. 1., *Medieval Drama*. Ed. A.C. Cawley et al., 152–206. London, 1983.

Munson, William F. 'Audience and Meaning in Two Medieval Dramatic Realisms.' In *The Drama of the Middle Ages*. Ed. Clifford Davidson, C.J. Giankaris, and John H. Stroupe, 183–206. New York, 1982.

– 'Holiday, Audience Participation, and Characterization in the Shepherds' Plays.' *Research Opportunities in Renaissance Drama* 15–16 (1972–3): 97–115.

Murdoch, Brian O. 'The Cornish Medieval Drama.' In *Cambridge Companion*. Ed. Beadle, 211–39.

Murphy, James J. *Rhetoric in the Middle Ages: A History of Rhetorical Theory from Saint Augustine to the Renaissance*. Berkeley, 1974.

Murphy, James, ed. *Three Medieval Rhetorical Arts*. Berkeley, 1971.

Murphy, Thomas Patrick. 'The Characters Called Corpus Christi: Dramatic Characterization in the English Mystery Cycles.' Diss. Ohio State U, 1975.

The N-Town Play: Cotton MS Vespasian D.8. Ed. Stephen Spector. 2 vols. EETS ss 11–12. Oxford, 1991.

The New Oxford Annotated Bible with the Apocrypha, Revised Standard Version, ed. Herbert G. May and Bruce M. Metzger. New York, 1977.

Non-Cycle Plays and Fragments. Ed. Norman Davis. EETS ss 1. London, 1970.

Owst, G.R. *Literature and Pulpit in Medieval England*. 2nd ed. Oxford, 1961.

Le Patronage de Saint Joseph: Actes du Congrès d'Études. Montreal, 1956.

Pentzell, Raymond J. 'The Medieval Theatre in the Streets.' *Theatre Survey* 14 (1973): 1–21.

Phythian-Adams, Charles. 'Ceremony and Citizen: The Communal Year at Coventry, 1450–1550.' In *Crisis and Order in English Towns*. Ed. Peter Clark and Paul Slack, pp. 57–85. Toronto, 1972.

Pizarro, Joaquin Martinez. *A Rhetoric of the Scene: Dramatic Narrative in the Early Middle Ages*. Toronto, 1989.

Prosser, Eleanor. *Drama and Religion in the English Mystery Plays: A Re-Evaluation*. Stanford, 1961.

Reinburg, Virginia. 'Praying to Saints in the Late Middle Ages.' In *Saints*. Ed. Sticca, 269–82.

Rhetorica ad Herennium. Ed. and trans. Harry Caplan. Loeb Classical Library 403. Cambridge, MA, 1954.

Ricke, Joseph M. 'Parody, Performance, and the "Ultimate" Meaning of Noah's Shrew,' *Mediaevalia* 18 (1995): 263–82.

Robert of Basevorn. *The Form of Preaching*. Trans. Leopold Krul. In *Three Medieval Rhetorical Arts*. Ed. Murphy, 109–216.

Robertson, D.W. Jr. *A Preface to Chaucer: Studies in Medieval Perspectives*. Princeton, NJ, 1962.

Robinson, J.W. 'A Commentary on the York Play of the Birth of Jesus.' *Journal of English and Germanic Philology* 70 (1971): 241–54.

Rondet, Henri. *Saint Joseph*. Ed. and trans. Donald Attwater. New York, 1956.

Ross, Woodburn O., ed. *Middle English Sermons*. EETS os 209. London, 1940.

Rossiaud, Jacques. *Medieval Prostitution*. Trans. Lydia G. Cochrane. London, 1988.

Rubin, Miri. *Corpus Christi: The Eucharist in Late Medieval Culture*. Cambridge, 1991.

Scherb, Victor I. 'Frame Structure in *The Conversion of Saint Paul*.' *Comparative Drama* 26 (1992): 124–39.

– 'Worldly and Sacred Messengers in the Digby *Mary Magdalene*.' *English Studies* 1 (1992): 1–9.

Scoville, Chester N. 'A Scribal Error in Townley Play 28.' *Notes and Queries*. New Series 47.3 (September 2000): 298–9.

Shinners, John, ed. *Medieval Popular Religion, 1000–1500: A Reader*. Readings in Medieval Civilizations and Cultures 11. Ser. Ed. Paul Edward Dutton. Peterborough, ON, 1997.

Skey, Miriam Anne. 'Herod the Great in Medieval European Drama.' *Comparative Drama* 10 (1976): 330–64.

Smith, Jadwiga S. 'The English Medieval Conversion Plays and the Doctrine of St. Augustine.' *Medieval Perspectives* 3 (1988): 242–51.

The South English Legendary. Ed. Charlotte D'Evelyn and Anna J. Mills. EETS os 235–6. London, 1956.

Specht, Henrik. '"Ethopoeia" or Impersonation: A Neglected Species of Medieval Characterization.' *Chaucer Review* 21 (1986): 1–15.

Staines, David. 'To Out-Herod Herod: The Development of Dramatic Character.' *Comparative Drama* 10 (1976), 29–53.

Stevens, Martin. *Four Middle English Mystery Cycles: Textual, Contextual, and Critical Interpretations.* Princeton, NJ, 1987.

– 'Herod as Carnival King in the Medieval Biblical Drama,' *Mediaevalia* 18 (1995): 43–66.

– 'Illusion and Reality in the Medieval Drama.' *College English* 32 (1971): 448–64.

– 'The Missing Parts of the Towneley Cycle.' *Speculum* 45 (1970): 254–65.

Sticca, Sandro, ed. *Saints: Studies in Hagiography.* Binghamton, 1996.

Taylor, Larissa. 'Sister, Whore, Apostle, Preacher: Images of Mary Magdalene in the Sermons and Art of the Late Middle Ages and Reformation.' U of Toronto, 22 Jan. 1998, lecture.

Thomas, Keith. *Religion and the Decline of Magic: Studies in Popular Beliefs in Sixteenth- and Seventeenth-Century England.* 1971. Repr. London, 1991.

Thomson, Peter. 'Rogues and Rhetoricians: Acting Styles in Early English Drama.' *A New History of Early English Drama.* Ed. John D. Cox and David Scott Kastan. New York, 1997. 321–36.

Tiner, Elza. 'Inventio, Distributio, and Elocutio in the York Trial Plays.' Diss. U of Toronto, 1987.

The Towneley Plays. Ed. Martin Stevens and A.C. Cawley. 2 Vols. EETS ss 13–14. Oxford, 1994.

Travis, Peter. 'Affective Criticism, the Pilgrimage of Reading, and Medieval English Literature.' In *Medieval Texts and Contemporary Readers.* Ed. Laurie A. Finke and Martin B. Shichtman, 201–15. Ithaca, NY, 1987.

A Tretise of Miraclis Pleyinge. Ed. Clifford Davidson. Early Art, Drama, and Music Monograph Series 19. Kalamazoo, 1993.

Two Coventry Corpus Christi Plays. Ed. Hardin Craig. 2nd Ed. EETS es 87. Oxford, 1952.

Twycross, Meg. 'The Theatricality of Medieval English Drama.' In *Cambridge Companion.* Ed. Beadle, 37–84.

Velz, John W. 'From Jerusalem to Damascus: Bilocal Dramaturgy in Medieval and Shakespearean Conversion Plays.' *Comparative Drama* 15 (1981–2): 311–26.

– 'Sovereignty in the Digby *Mary Magdalene.*' *Comparative Drama* 2 (1968): 32–43.

Vinter, Donna Smith. 'Didactic Characterization: The Towneley Abraham.' *Comparative Drama* 14 (1980): 117–36.

Wall, Carolyn. 'The Apocryphal and Historical Backgrounds of "The Appearance of Our Lady to Thomas" (Play XLVI of the York Cycle).' *Mediaeval Studies* 32 (1970): 172–92.

Walsh, Martin. 'Divine Cuckold / Holy Fool: The Comic Image of Joseph in the English "Troubles" Play.' In *England and the Fourteenth Century: Proceedings of the 1985 Harlaxton Symposium*. Ed. W.M. Ormrod, 278–97. Woodbridge, 1986.

Warner, Marina. *Alone of All Her Sex: The Myth and the Cult of the Virgin Mary*. 1976. Repr. New York, 1983.

Wickham, Glynne. 'The Staging of Saint Plays in England.' In *The Medieval Drama*. Ed. Sandro Sticca, 99–119. Albany, 1972.

Williams, Arnold. *The Characterization of Pilate in the Towneley Cycle*. East Lansing, 1950.

– 'The Comic in the Cycles.' In *Medieval Drama*. Ed. Denny, 108–23.

Wilson, Thomas. *The Art of Rhetoric*. 1560. Ed. Peter E. Medine. U Park, 1994.

Woolf, Rosemary. *The English Mystery Plays*. London, 1972.

Yates, Frances. *The Art of Memory*. Chicago, 1966.

The York Play: A Facsimile of British Library MS Additional 35290, Together with a Facsimile of the Ordo Paginarum Section of the A/Y Memorandum Book. Ed. Richard Beadle and Peter Meredith. Leeds, 1983.

The York Plays. Ed. Richard Beadle. York Medieval Texts. 2nd Series. London, 1982.

York Plays: The Plays Performed by the Crafts or Mysteries of York on the Day of Corpus Christi in the 14th, 15th, and 16th Centuries. Ed. Lucy Toulmin Smith. 1885. Repr. New York, 1963.

Young, Karl. *The Drama of the Medieval Church*. Oxford, 1933.

Index